T0368329

Journey through Life

Our Earthly Journey with Jesus Paralleled with Israel's Wilderness Journey with God

Devotionals by: Randy A. Christianson

WestBow Press books may be ordered through booksellers or by contacting:

WestBow Press
A Division of Thomas Nelson & Zondervan
1663 Liberty Drive
Bloomington, IN 47403
www.westbowpress.com
1 (866) 928-1240

To learn more about devotionals or Randy Christianson go to www.rachristianson.com

ISBN: 978-1-9736-9152-5 (sc)
ISBN: 978-1-9736-9153-2 (e)

Library of Congress Control Number: 2020909145

Print information available on the last page.

WestBow Press rev. date: 7/30/2020

WESTBOW
P R E S S®
A DIVISION OF THOMAS NELSON
& ZONDERVAN

Randy A. Christianson is a devoted husband, father, grandfather, friend, and mentor. From a young age, he has been interested in studying God's Word. His mother told him that during worship services, he would have his eyes fixed on the pastor, intently listening and learning.

As an adult, he developed a passion for teaching others about God's Word and how to have a personal relationship with Jesus Christ. He has led and taught Bible studies for over thirty years, all the while keeping notes from those studies. He uses those notes to write Christ-centered devotionals.

His simple writing style brings clarity and understanding to the reader.

Melissa W.

I found the parallels between the Exodus and the book of John intriguing. He seemed to follow the chronology of Exodus, finding the corollary or parallel in John's gospel. Very interesting. Saw some ties I had not noticed before.

Pastor John K.

Future devotionals, the Lord willing, are these:

-God's Plan of Salvation (Salvation from God Alone)
-The Christian Life (Abiding *in Christ*)
-Summary of the Law (Made New *in Christ*)
-Fruit of the Spirit (New Testament Fulfillment of Old Testament Ten Commandments)
-Old Covenant vs. New Covenant (Works vs. Grace)
-Christ's Obedience in Your Heart ('Free' Will or Obedience to God's Will)
-Isaiah (The Bible Consolidated into One Book)

Table of Contents

Introduction 1

List of Devotionals 2

Devotionals.. 4

Jacob's Family in Egypt (Seventy Persons) and in the Exodus (Seventy Family Units Leaving Egypt) 56

Forty Camps Time Line 58

Afterwords.. 60

Introduction

While reading the book of John, I saw references to Moses' and Israel's wilderness journey from Egypt to Canaan and began to see parallels between their journey in the wilderness and our journey in the world. I came up with fifty-five parallels (and I am sure there are more), and narrowed them down to fifty-two, one devotional a week for a year. (If you prefer, this devotional booklet can also be used as a daily devotional.)

Each devotional is divided into five sections: Israel's Wilderness Journey with God, Our Earthly Journey with Jesus, What about You?, Prayer, and Verse of the Week/Day. There are highlighted words in the verse(s) under the Israel's Wilderness Journey with God and the What about You? sections. These show the parallels between what the Bible says about Israel's journey and our journey.

Our Earthly Journey with Jesus is based on scripture from the gospel of John. Each devotional also has a word or words with the meaning arising from a biblical perspective under the section What about You? and ends with a prayer and a weekly/daily scripture that summarizes the devotional.

I pray you will be inspired!

List of Devotionals

Israel's Wilderness Journey with God
(From Slaves of Egypt to Freedom in Canaan)

> "You have seen what I [the LORD] did to the Egyptians, and how I bore you [Israel] on eagles' wings and brought you to Myself."
> —Exodus 19:4

1) Slaves of Egypt
2) God's Will Accomplished Through Moses
3) God's Love for Israel—Sent Moses
4) Moses Was Humble—An Empty Vessel
5) Pharaoh Resisted God's Message —Oppression Increased
6) Signs and Wonders—Plagues
7) God Freed Israel—Received Favor from Egypt
8) Pillar of Cloud/Fire—Guide by Day and Night
9) Israel Passed through by Wind/Water
10) Victory over Foe—Egyptians
11) Salvation from God Alone
12) Believed by Faith
13) New Life Journey into the Wilderness
14) Tested on Their Journey
15) God Used a Tree to Draw Israel to Himself
16) Faith Walk Based on Obedience —God Alone Heals
17) A Brief Rest on the Journey
18) Manna—Bread from Heaven
19) God's Manna Came Daily—Test of Faith
20) Manna—Gather before the Heat of the Day
21) Rephidim—Struggle Against/Tempting God
22) Water from the Rock Quenches Thirst
23) Elders Witnessed Striking the Rock
24) Enemy Attacked When Least Expected
25) Moses Depending on the Flesh
26) Moses' Brothers Help Him
27) Aaron: Priest/Intercessor
    Hur: Noble/Blameless

Our Earthly Journey with Jesus
(From Slaves of Sin to Freedom *in Christ*)

> He [Jesus], bearing His cross, went out to … the Place of a Skull —John 19:17
> Jesus … said, "I … will draw all peoples [nations] to Myself." —John 12:30–32

1) Slaves of Sin
2) God's Will Accomplished Through Jesus
3) God's Love for Us—Sent Jesus
4) Jesus Humbled—Emptied Himself
5) Pharisees Resisted Jesus' Message —Oppression Increased
6) Signs and Wonders—Miracles
7) Jesus Freed Us—Received Favor from God
8) The Holy Spirit—Guide by Day and Night
9) We Pass through by Spirit/Water
10) Victory over Foe—Sin and Death
11) Salvation from God Alone
12) Believe by Faith
13) New Life Journey into the World
14) Tested on Our Journey
15) God Uses a Tree/Cross to Draw Us to Jesus
16) Faith Walk Based on Obedience —Jesus Alone Heals
17) A Brief Rest on Our Journey
18) Jesus—Bread from Heaven
19) Jesus is Our *Daily Bread*—Test of Faith
20) Prayer—Food before the *Heat of the Day*
21) No Trust—Struggle Against/Tempting Jesus
22) Water from *the Rock* Quenches Thirst
23) Sanhedrin Witnessed Striking *the Rock*
24) Enemy Attacks When Least Expected
25) Depending on Our Own Strength
26) Helping Our Brothers and Sisters
27) Jesus: Priest/Intercessor
    Jesus: Righteous/Blameless

Israel's Wilderness Journey with God (From Slaves of Egypt to Freedom in Canaan)	**Our Earthly Journey with Jesus** (From Slaves of Sin to Freedom *in Christ*)
"You have seen what I [the LORD] did to the Egyptians, and how I bore you [Israel] on eagles' wings and brought you to Myself." —Exodus 19:4	He [Jesus], bearing His cross, went out to … the Place of a Skull —John 19:17 Jesus … said, "I … will draw all peoples [nations] to Myself." —John 12:30–32

28) Jethro Drawn to God through Witness	28) Others Drawn to God through Witness
29) Testimony of God's Power	29) Testimony of Christ's Power
30) Moses Acknowledges His Weakness	30) Confessing Our Weaknesses/Sin
31) God's Advice—Seventy Judges —Filled with the Spirit	31) Jesus' Advice—Follow Me —Be Filled with the Spirit
32) Through Moses—God Chose Israel to Be Holy	32) Through Jesus—God Chose Us to be Holy
33) Israel Responsible for Its Disobedience —God's Mercy	33) Responsible for Our Disobedience —Jesus' Mercy
34) Israel Belonged to God —No Covenants with Canaan	34) We Belong to Jesus —No Covenants with the World
35) Moses Taught the People God's Word	35) Jesus Teaches Us His Word
36) Serving God Wholeheartedly	36) Serving Jesus Wholeheartedly
37) Israel Designed the Tabernacle for Worship	37) Jesus Designed the Heart for Worship
38) The Sacrificial Lamb—No Broken Bones	38) Jesus, the Sacrificial Lamb—No Broken Bones
39) Ark Embodied God's Presence —Follow the Ark/God	39) Jesus Embodies God's Presence —Follow the Spirit/Jesus
40) Rabble/Rebels—Children of Unknown Fathers	40) Barabbas/Rebellious—Son of Unknown Father
41) Joshua/Caleb Report—Victory Foretold	41) Disciple Report—Victory Foretold
42) Spent Forty Years in the Wilderness	42) Spend a Lifetime in a Sinful World
43) Speak to the Rock to Quench Thirst	43) Words of Eternal Life Quench Thirst
44) Moses—Out of Anger—Struck the Rock	44) Our Way—Anger—Bad Testimony
45) Israel Sins—God Sent Biting Serpents	45) We Sin—God Allows the Serpent to Bite
46) Look at the Snake for Healing —Snakes Not Removed	46) Look to the Cross for Healing —Not Removed from the World
47) Israel Was Blessed—Could not be Cursed	47) For Those Who Are Blessed—No Curse
48) Two and a Half Tribes Stayed in the Wilderness	48) Some Want to Stay Back in the World
49) God's Promises on Israel's Journey	49) God's Promises on Our Journey
50) Obedience—Response to God's Promises	50) Obedience—Response to God's Promises
51) New Generation Blessed with Canaan	51) Future Generations Blessed with Abundant Life
52) God Carried Israel to the End	52) Jesus Carries Us to the End

Devotional 1
Israel's Wilderness Journey with God (Slaves of Egypt)
> The children of Israel groaned because of the bondage, and they cried out; and their cry came up to God. ... God heard their groaning, and God remembered his covenant with Abraham, with Isaac, and with Jacob. And God looked upon the children of Israel, and God acknowledged [answered] them. —Exodus 2:23–25

When the children of Israel first came to Egypt, they were given the land of Goshen, which was the best the world had to offer then. It had the best land, food, wealth, and ease of life. But it was not long before the Egyptians put them in bondage. After two hundred eighty years of slavery, the Israelites cried out to the LORD* for deliverance. He heard their cries for help and remembered the promise He made to their ancestors, Abraham, Isaac, and Jacob. He planned to deliver them from their physical bondage as well as deliver them from their spiritual bondage, the slavery of sin. *(Capital L-O-R-D is Jesus/Yahweh in the Old Testament)

Our Earthly Journey with Jesus (Slaves of Sin)
> Jesus said, ... "If you abide in My Word, you are My disciples indeed. And you shall know the truth, and the truth shall make you free." They answered Him, "We are Abraham's descendants, and have never been in bondage to anyone. How can You say, 'you will be made free'?" Jesus answered them, "Most assuredly I say to you, whoever commits sin is a slave of sin." —John 8:31–34

Jesus was telling the Jews who were following Him that they were in bondage and needed His Word to be set free. But they disagreed, saying they were Abraham's descendants and not slaves. They did not understand Him when He said they needed to be set free by the Truth because they were thinking physically, not spiritually. Jesus was not talking about the physical relationship they had with Abraham but about their spiritual condition concerning slavery to sin and their broken relationship with God. Only Jesus, the Truth, can set humanity free from the bondage/slavery of sin.

What about You?
The word *groan* means "to inwardly desire relief from your sinful condition." This world has a lot to offer, but it eventually leads to emptiness, disappointment, failure, and bondage. Does sin cause you to groan inwardly and cry to God for help? If you are convicted of sin, regardless of whether you are a Christian or one who is seeking salvation and forgiveness; God will hear your groaning, He will remember His promise to you, He will look upon you with compassion, and He will answer your cry for relief from your sinful condition.

Prayer
Father in heaven, we live in a world that has a lot to offer us, but it leads only to emptiness, disappointment, failure, and bondage. Through Your Holy Spirit, who convicts us of sin, hear our groaning, remember Your promises to us, look upon us with compassion, and answer our cry for relief from our sinful condition. We need Jesus to set us free. In Jesus' name we pray, amen.

Verse of the Week/Day
> ... The whole creation groans and labors with birth pangs together until now. ... We also ... groan within ourselves, eagerly waiting for the adoption. ... The Spirit Himself makes intercession for us with groanings which cannot be uttered ... according to the will of God. —Romans 8:22–27

Devotional 2
Israel's Wilderness Journey with God (God's Will Accomplished Through Moses)

> Moses said, "I will now turn aside and see this great sight, why the bush does not burn." The LORD saw that he turned aside to look, so God called to him from the midst of the bush and said, "Moses, Moses." And he said, "Here I am." —Exodus 3:3–4

When God prepared to deliver Israel, He chose Moses to be His instrument. He wanted to do His will in and through Moses. Moses had come from being a prince in the palace of Egypt, an heir to the throne of one of the most powerful nations on earth, to a lowly, desolate place in the desert of Midian to take care of sheep. While Moses was far from home caring for sheep belonging to Jethro, his father-in-law, God caught Moses' attention through a bush on fire but not consumed. When he reached the burning bush, the voice of the LORD (Yahweh/Jesus) called out to him. Moses responded, "Here I am."

Our Earthly Journey with Jesus (God's Will Accomplished Through Jesus)

> Jesus said, "I am the Bread of Life. He [the one] who comes to Me shall never hunger, and he [the one] who believes in [on (KJV)] Me shall never thirst." … "All that the Father gives Me will come to Me, and the one who comes to Me I will by no means cast out. For I have come down from heaven, not to do My own will, but the will of Him who sent Me." —John 6:35–38

Before the beginning of time, God prepared the deliverance of His people from sin. The same Jesus (the LORD of the Old Testament—Yahweh) who chose Moses to be the instrument to deliver Israel from the bondage of Egypt became God's instrument to deliver His people from the bondage of sin. God, the Father, chose Jesus, the Son, to leave His place of glory and come down to this lowly, sinful earth to accomplish the Father's will—dying on the cross to pay for our sin so we could be forgiven and receive eternal life.

What about You?

The word *called* means "chosen for a divine purpose, a divine summons, a command." Through the power of the Holy Spirit, God has called/chosen you to be His instrument for His divine purpose.

God called Moses from the burning bush to deliver Israel from the bondage of Egypt. Moses responded, "Here I am." God called Jesus before the beginning of time to deliver us from the bondage of sin. Jesus responded, "Here I am" (Hebrews 10:7 NIV). God wants to accomplish His will in and through you also. He is calling you, His instrument, to share His Word with the world. You must respond, "Here I am."

Prayer

Father, Your Word says that this world needs the gospel, the good news of Jesus, so it can be saved from the bondage of sin. Through Jesus, Your Word, and the power of the Holy Spirit, I hear Your divine summons to be Your instrument. I know that You want to accomplish Your will in and through me. My answer is, "Here I am." In Jesus' name, amen.

Verse of the Week/Day

> The LORD called Samuel. He answered, "Here I am!" So, he ran to Eli and said, "Here I am, for you called me." … Then Eli perceived that the LORD had called the boy. Therefore, Eli said to Samuel, … "If He calls you, … you must say, 'Speak LORD, for Your servant hears.' " —1 Samuel 3:4–10

Devotional 3
Israel's Wilderness Journey with God (God's Love for Israel—Sent Moses)
>The LORD said: "I have surely seen the oppression of My people who are in Egypt, and have heard their cry because of their taskmasters, for I know their sorrows. So I have come down to deliver them." … "Come now, … I [the LORD] will send you [Moses] to Pharaoh that you may bring My people, the children of Israel, out of Egypt."
>—Exodus 3:7–10

God loved the children of Israel with a deep love, a love that shared in their sorrow and misery, a love that caused Him to respond with compassion to their cry for help. He was fulfilling the promise He had made to Abraham to bring his descendants back to Canaan, a land flowing with milk and honey. God came down to deliver His people from their oppression, but He was sending Moses to Pharaoh as His instrument to bring His people out of Egypt.

Our Earthly Journey with Jesus (God's Love for Us—Sent Jesus)
>For God so loved the world that He gave His only begotten Son [Jesus]. —John 3:16a

A paraphrase of this verse could be, "God so loved sinners, those in bondage/slavery to sin, that He sent His Son, Jesus Christ, to rescue them." God's love for sinners (us) was so great that He was willing to give us His only Son to shoulder our sorrow and misery (which Jesus knew intimately because He took on our humanity) and bring us out of the slavery of sin. To save us from sin, Jesus first had to remain God—perfect, holy, and sinless—to bear the wrath of God against our sin. Second, Jesus had to become a man—a human instrument—in order for us to know the love of God and to pay the penalty of our sin—death on the cross, a penalty we could not pay ourselves.

What about You?
To *send* means "to cause to go, to be commissioned." God has chosen men and women to be His instruments, to accomplish His will in and through them. Here are some examples: Adam named the animals, prophets brought God's Word, parents teach their children, the Bible was written by people through the inspiration of the Holy Spirit—we could go on and on.

In the last devotional, we talked about God's call and your response to be His instrument. Now He wants to use you. In other words, an instrument can do nothing on its own; it must have someone (Jesus) to play it. He does not send you out on your own, but through the Holy Spirit, He has chosen to work in and through you to accomplish His will. God loves the world deeply, so He sends you, a human instrument played by Him, to bring the world out of sin's bondage back to Him.

Prayer
Father in heaven, I am Your instrument. Send me. Pick me up and work in and through me by the power of the Holy Spirit to bring the world back to You so that it can be released from the bondage of sin and brought to complete freedom *in Christ*. Thank You for loving us so much that You were willing to give us Jesus to save us from sin. In His name we pray, amen.

Verse of the Week/Day
>So I [Isaiah] said, "Woe is me, for I am … a man of unclean lips." … Then one of the seraphim [an angel] flew to me, having in his hand a live coal. … He touched my mouth with it: … "your iniquity is taken away, and your sin purged." Also, I heard the voice of the LORD, saying: "Whom shall I send?" … Then I said, "Here I am! Send me." —Isaiah 6:5–8

Devotional 4
Israel's Wilderness Journey with God (Moses Was Humble—An Empty Vessel)

> Moses said to God, "Who am I that I should go to Pharaoh, and … bring the children of Israel out of Egypt?" So He [God] said, "I will certainly be with you." Then Moses said to God, … "When I … say to them, 'The God of your fathers has sent me to you,' and they say … 'What is His name?' What shall I say?" … God said to Moses, "I AM WHO I AM." —Exodus 3:11–14

Moses asked God, "Who am I?" Did he think he was unworthy? Was he afraid of confronting Pharaoh? Did he doubt he would be able to carry out this task? God assured him that He was certainly going to be with him and gave him the sign that when the Israelites would be brought out of Egypt, He would bring them back to the very place where they were speaking, to worship Him.

Moses was also concerned about the people of Israel receiving his message from God. So God told him to tell them He was the Great I AM, the God of Abraham, Isaac, and Jacob. Moses was a prince in Egypt his first forty years, and then he fled to the wilderness and was a lowly shepherd for the next forty years. Moses did not know that God had been preparing him the whole time to become the humble leader of Israel. In Numbers 12:3, we read that Moses was very humble, more than any other person on earth. Moses was I AM's humble vessel prepared and enabled by God to deliver Israel.

Our Earthly Journey with Jesus (Jesus Humbled—Emptied Himself)

> "I am the Good Shepherd. The Good Shepherd gives [lays down] His life for the sheep. … Other sheep I have which are not of this fold; them also I must bring, and they will hear My voice; and there will be one flock and one shepherd. … I lay down My life that I may take it again. No one takes it from Me, but I lay it down of Myself."
> —John 10:11–18

Jesus humbled/emptied Himself obediently even to death on the cross. He laid down His life for His sheep. He lovingly emptied His life into us, His own, so we could know Him and be saved.

What about You?

The word *humble* means "to empty/submit." Are you afraid of bringing God's message of salvation to the world? Are you afraid the world will not receive the message? Are you afraid you might be ridiculed and even persecuted? Do not be afraid, God promises to be with you wherever you go. Like Moses, God will empty you of yourself and fill you with Jesus, the Great I AM. Then with the Holy Spirit as your constant, faithful companion, you can go into the world equipped to deliver God's message of salvation.

Prayer

Father in heaven, we humbly ask You to empty us of our sinful ways and fill us with the Great I AM, Jesus Christ. Thank you that we are not on our own, but by Your Holy Spirit, You are always with us. Help us not to be afraid when we deliver the message of salvation that You have put in our hearts to communicate to the world. In Jesus' name we pray, amen.

Verse of the Week/Day

> I am crucified with Christ: nevertheless I live; yet not I, but Christ lives in me: … the life which I now live in the flesh I live by the faith of the Son of God, who loved me and gave Himself for me. —Galatians 2:20 (KJV)

Devotional 5
Israel's Wilderness Journey with God (Pharaoh Resisted God's Message—Oppression Increased)

> Moses and Aaron … told Pharaoh, "Thus says the LORD God of Israel; Let My people go, that they may hold a feast to [worship] Me in the wilderness." Pharaoh said, "Who is the LORD, that I should obey His voice to let Israel go? … Let more work be laid on the men." —Exodus 5:1–9

Moses and Aaron, instruments of God, were filled with His Holy Spirit. God sent them and spoke through them telling Pharaoh to let the people go so they could worship Him in the wilderness. But Pharaoh resisted the LORD's message because he did not know Him. Moses had been afraid that Pharaoh would not listen to their message from God. To make it worse, Pharaoh increased the oppression of the children of Israel by ordering them to find their own straw—which had been provided for them—and make the same amount of bricks as before or be beaten even to the point of death.

To add insult to injury, the Israelites came against Moses and Aaron for the extra work that was laid on them. They were so angry that they no longer listened to them. Despite the opposition, God told Moses and Aaron that He had not forgotten His promise to them and the Israelites. He was about to show His power against Pharaoh and bring judgment against the Egyptians for resisting His message.

Our Earthly Journey with Jesus (Pharisees Resisted Jesus' Message—Oppression Increased)

> Many of the Jews who had come to Mary, and had seen the things Jesus did, believed in [on (KJV)] Him. … The chief priests and the Pharisees gathered a council and said, "What shall we do? For this Man works many signs." … From that day on, they plotted to put Him to death. —John 11:45–53

Jesus, God's Word, was the instrument that God sent to this world to redeem His people. He too was filled with the Holy Spirit, God's Power, and had just raised Lazarus back to life. Many who witnessed this miracle believed on Him. But others, including the Pharisees and the high priest, resisted Him because they did not know who Jesus really was. They thought He was trying to take over the Jewish nation, plus their roles of leadership, and were afraid all the people would soon be following Him. From that day forward, they planned to get rid of Jesus even if it meant killing Him.

What about You?

The word *oppression* means "persecution, harassment." God sends you—filled with the Holy Spirit—to bring His powerful Word to others. But, as God's instrument, you will face oppression. The world will resist God's message and ask, "Who is Jesus that we should obey Him?"

Prayer

Father in heaven, work in and through us by Your Spirit, though we might experience oppression, to bring Your Word to this evil world. We know You are faithful in keeping Your promises and will surely be with us. In Jesus' name we pray, amen.

Verse of the Week/Day

> Jesus came and spoke to them saying, "All authority has been given to Me in heaven and on earth. Go therefore and make disciples of all the nations, baptizing them in the name of the Father, … the Son, and … the Holy Spirit, teaching them to observe all things that I have commanded you; … I am with you always, even to the end of the age." —Matthew 28:18–20

Devotional 6
Israel's Wilderness Journey with God (Signs and Wonders—Plagues)
> The LORD said to Moses, … "You shall speak all that I command you, … and I will harden Pharaoh's heart and will multiply My signs and My wonders in the land of Egypt. … The Egyptians shall know that I am the LORD, when I stretch out My hand on Egypt and bring out the children of Israel from among them." —Exodus 7:1–5

This passage is where God began to show Pharaoh and the Egyptians who He really was, the LORD of heaven and earth. All through these devotionals, you will see that God is all-powerful and always in control of all things—that He is sovereign.

God chose to make Himself known; speaking and acting (stretching out His hand) through Moses and Aaron—His instruments. God used Moses and Aaron so the Egyptians would know, understand, and believe that the LORD was not only the all-powerful God of heaven and earth, but also the personal God of the Israelites, whom He was about to bring out of Egypt.

God hardened Pharaoh's heart by displaying His power and sending judgment on Pharaoh and the Egyptians through ten signs and wonders—the overpowering plagues—that Pharaoh (who thought of himself as the all-powerful king) could not overcome.

Our Earthly Journey with Jesus (Signs and Wonders—Miracles)
> A certain nobleman whose son was sick … went to Him [Jesus] and implored Him to … heal his son. … Then Jesus said to him, "Unless you people see signs and wonders, you will by no means believe." The nobleman said, … "Sir, come down before my child dies!" Jesus said, … "Go your way; your son lives." So the man believed the Word that Jesus spoke to him, and went his way. —John 4:46–50

God performed miracles (supernatural acts) through Jesus. Jesus took on human flesh so that we might know, understand, and believe on Him. The nobleman in this passage asked Jesus to come to his house and heal his son. Instead, Jesus healed the nobleman's son with His spoken Word. The son was cured that hour. God caused this man to believe just by hearing Jesus' Word. God's Word is all-powerful and miraculous. At creation (Genesis 1), God spoke, and the heavens and the earth came into being out of nothing. God's Word, Jesus Christ, has the power to create, to heal, to transform, and to save.

What about You?
Plagues and *miracles* are divinely ordained acts. God's powerful Word alone either softens or hardens peoples' hearts. As you—His instrument—bring His Word to the world, those with hard hearts will resist God's Word, but those whose hearts He softens, God miraculously produces faith, repentance, and the knowledge that Jesus is their Lord and Savior.

Prayer
Lord Jesus, show Your signs and wonders. By Your all-powerful Word, speak and act through us, Your instruments, so those we come in contact with may miraculously know and believe You are also their Lord and Savior. In Your name we pray, amen.

Verse of the Week/Day
> "… I [the king] thought it good to declare the signs and wonders that the Most High God has worked [performed] for me. How great are His signs, and how mighty His wonders! His kingdom is an everlasting kingdom, and His dominion is from generation to generation." —Daniel 4:2–3

Devotional 7
Israel's Wilderness Journey with God (God Freed Israel—Received Favor from Egypt)

> The Egyptians urged the people, that they might send them out of the land in haste. For they said, "We shall all be dead." … Now the children of Israel … asked from the Egyptians articles of silver, articles of gold, and clothing. The LORD had given the people favor in the sight of the Egyptians, so that they granted them what they requested. Thus, they plundered the Egyptians. —Exodus 12:33–36

Pharaoh would not listen to, much less obey, God's command to let the children of Israel go. So with the last plague, God sent His angel to destroy the firstborn of every family including Pharaoh's. Pharaoh and the Egyptians were defeated, and urged the children of Israel to leave the land before they all died.

But before the Israelites left Egypt, the LORD gave the people favor in the sight of the Egyptians. The Egyptians gave them everything they asked for and needed without questioning them and then drove them out of the land. The Israelites were no longer slaves but were free from the bondage of Egypt with the provisions they needed for the journey they were about to begin with God's family.

Our Earthly Journey with Jesus (Jesus Freed Us—Received Favor from God)

> Jesus answered them, … "A slave does not abide in the house forever, but a son [the Son (KJV)] abides forever. Therefore, if the Son makes you free, you shall be free indeed." —John 8:34–36

In the physical world, a *slave/servant/employee* is not a member of the family and will not receive an inheritance. Thus, if we are slaves of sin, we would not be members of God's family and would not inherit eternal life. We would eventually be removed from God's presence and suffer eternal separation from Him and His family. For us to have favor with God and become His children, God needed to free us from sin. Only through the sacrifice of Christ on the cross did we receive that freedom. Jesus poured His life and gifts into us so we would have everything we needed to live in obedience to Him and receive the inheritance—life in the presence of God and his family forever. That is true freedom indeed!

What about You?

The word *favor* means "grace/kindness." Because Christ freed you from the penalty of sin, you are no longer a slave to it. You did not merit or earn your salvation, but by grace—unmerited kindness—God has found favor with you in His sight. Because of the shedding of Jesus' blood on the cross and His resurrection from the dead, He now sees Jesus in you and not your sin.

Prayer

Father in heaven, because of Your favor, You no longer see our sin but Jesus in us. By grace, You have forgiven us, freed us from the penalty of sin, and have given us everything we need to live lives of obedience to Your will. Because of Your kindness, You have also given us the inheritance of life eternal with You and Your family. We are so thankful! In Jesus' name we pray, amen.

Verse of the Week/Day

> LORD, You have been favorable to Your land; You have brought back the captivity of Jacob. You have forgiven the iniquity of Your people; You have covered all their sin. … Show us Your mercy LORD, and grant us Your salvation. —Psalm 85:1–7

Devotional 8
Israel's Wilderness Journey with God (Pillar of Cloud and Fire—Guide by Day and Night)

> The LORD went before them by day in a pillar of cloud to lead the way, and by night in a pillar of fire to give them light. … He did not take away the pillar of cloud by day or the pillar of fire by night from before the people.
>
> —Exodus 13:21–22

It was four hundred thirty years since Jacob and Israel's ancestors had come to Egypt from Canaan. They were not far from Canaan and could have journeyed there in a week or two, but God had a different plan. He brought them the long way around through the wilderness to display His power and show that they needed to depend on Him alone for all their needs; physical and spiritual.

In those days, there were very few paved roads and no lighted cities to brighten the night skies. So the LORD (Yahweh/Jesus) went before them to lead the way and give them light. Through His servant Moses, He guided them, showing His presence with a cloud that led them during the day and was a cover from the sun's heat; and a cloud of fire by night so they had warmth and light. God's presence never left them throughout their journey to Canaan.

Our Earthly Journey with Jesus (The Holy Spirit—Guide by Day and Night)

> Jesus said, "I am the Light of the world. Whoever follows Me will never walk in darkness." —John 8:12 (NIV)

> "I am the Way, the Truth, and the Life. … I will pray to the Father, and He will give you another Helper, that He may abide with you forever, the Spirit of Truth. … You know Him, for He dwells with you and will be in you."
>
> —John 14:6–17

When Jesus told His disciples that He would soon leave them, they were troubled. Jesus assured them that He would be with them and lead them after He left earth by sending them His Holy Spirit, who would continually guide them day and night on their journey and bring into remembrance all He had taught them. He would dwell with them and His presence would be in them, giving them light and direction throughout their journey here on earth and beyond, for all eternity.

What about You?

Guide means "to give direction, to enlighten." Jesus, the Way, the Truth, the Life, and the Light of world is in you. After He saved you from your sin, He did not send you out on your own but gave you His Holy Spirit, who will never leave you. He will go before you day and night to give you direction and enlightenment every step of the way, so you do not stray from God, but obey Him in everything. Do not be troubled; His Spirit is guiding you.

Prayer

Lord Jesus, we need You to lead and guide us each day along the pathway of this journey, so we do not stray from You ever. Thank You for leading us down life's path and giving us the light of Your presence in this dark world through the direction and enlightenment of Your Holy Spirit. Fill us with Your Way, Your Truth, and Your Life, so that You shine in and through us to bring others from the bondage of sin to salvation *in You*. In Your name we pray, amen.

Verse of the Week/Day

> Your Word is a lamp to my feet, and a light to my path. —Psalm 119:105

Devotional 9
Israel's Wilderness Journey with God (Israel Passed through by Wind/Water)

> Then Moses stretched out his hand over the sea; and the LORD caused the sea to go back by a strong east wind all that night, and made the sea into dry land, and the waters were divided. So the children of Israel went through the midst of the sea. —Exodus 14:21–22

The LORD caused the Red Sea to open by His breath—the Holy Spirit—and the children of Israel passed through the water (baptism) by faith. As they walked, they heard the wind (the invisible/spiritual part) and saw the water (the visible/physical part). In 1 Corinthians 10:1–4, we read that through Moses, their appointed leader, all were under the cloud, all passed through the sea, all were baptized, and all ate and drank the same spiritual food. Through God's almighty power and through His instrument, Moses' leadership, they were from this point on, in union with the LORD and part of His eternal kingdom.

Our Earthly Journey with Jesus (We Pass through by Spirit/Water)

> Jesus answered, "Most assuredly, I say to you, unless one is born of water and the Spirit, he cannot enter the kingdom of God. … The wind blows where it wishes, and you hear the sound of it, but cannot tell where it comes from and where it goes. So is everyone who is born of the Spirit." —John 3:5–8

Nicodemus came to Jesus by night and praised Him for His miraculous acts, but Jesus told him it was not enough to believe on Him for His miracles only. He had to by faith believe that He was his Savior from sin and be baptized by the Holy Spirit (the inward sign), and by water (the outward sign).

The Holy Spirit moved Nicodemus to come to Jesus for salvation. Later on, through Jesus' ministry, we see that Nicodemus had become a follower of Christ, defending Jesus' claim of being the Messiah in John 7 and helping with Jesus' burial after the crucifixion in John 19.

What about You?

The words *pass through* mean "to move from one place into another." Before Israel went through the Red Sea, Moses told the people to be still and watch what God was going to do. Instead, God urged Moses and Israel to obediently move forward based on His past faithfulness. (See Exodus 14:13–15.)

God is working through you to share Jesus with others so that they pass from death to life. For people to be *in Christ*, God first baptizes them spiritually (the inward sign) by the Holy Spirit (wind). Second, He causes them to walk by the faith of Christ through the baptism of water (the outward sign). God's faithfulness will cause them to obey and pass through boldly.

Prayer

Father in heaven, thank you for baptizing us by Your Spirit (spiritually) and by water (physically). Work through us to cause others to be moved by the wind of your Holy Spirit so that they pass through from death to life. In Jesus' name we pray, amen.

Verse of the Week/Day

> Peter said, … "Repent, and let every one of you be baptized in the Name of Jesus Christ for the remission of sins; and you shall receive the gift of the Holy Spirit. For the promise is to you and to your children, and to all who are far off, as many as the Lord our God will call." —Acts 2:38–39

Devotional 10
Israel's Wilderness Journey with God (Victory over Foe—Egyptians)

> The Egyptians pursued and went after them. … Then the LORD said to Moses, "Stretch out your hand over the sea, that the waters may come back upon the Egyptians." … So, the LORD overthrew the Egyptians in the midst of the sea and the waters returned, and covered … all the army of Pharaoh. Not so much as one of them remained. —Exodus 14:23–28

Pharaoh and the Egyptian army would not give up even after all the plagues and devastation God had brought upon Egypt. Shortly after the Israelites left Egypt, Pharaoh and the Egyptians realized that their workforce had left. They had been given the opportunity to believe on the LORD, but they rejected Him.

The Egyptians pursued the Israelites and caught up to them just before they crossed the Red Sea. God was watching over His people and put Himself between them and the Egyptians with light on the Israelites' side and darkness on the Egyptians' side. Because evil is persistent, the Egyptians followed Israel into the sea. When the army was in the midst of the sea, the LORD overthrew them through His instrument, Moses, and the walls of water collapsed on the Egyptians, destroying them.

Our Earthly Journey with Jesus (Victory Over Foe—Sin and Death)

> "He [the one] who hears My [Jesus'] Word and believes Him [the Father] who sent Me has everlasting life, and shall not come into judgment, but has passed from death into life. … The hour is coming, and now is, when the [spiritually] dead will hear the voice of the Son of God; and those who hear will live." —John 5:24–25

Only God by the Holy Spirit could have opened our dead hearts to hear the voice of Jesus calling to believe on Him and live. Through Jesus, God gave us complete victory over sin and death. Because we have passed from death to life, we will never have to face judgment for our sin. God has already judged/punished sin through His Son. We now have eternal life through God's Word, Jesus Christ.

What about You?

Victory means "overcoming an enemy." The penalty for sin is death—separation from God forever. But God overcame persistent sin and death, your greatest enemy, by sending His Son, Jesus Christ, to die on the cross in your place. Not so much as one of your sins remain or can come against you again. Because your sin has been destroyed, you have passed from eternal death to eternal life. This is the victorious message He sends you, with the Holy Spirit's power, to tell the world.

Prayer

Father in heaven, help us to tell others that because of sin, they are eternally separated from God and without hope. Then help us share the good news that You overcame sin and death through Jesus' suffering on the cross and resurrection from the dead, and that when they believe on Him, they will have complete victory over sin and death and receive eternal life. In Jesus' name we pray, amen.

Verse of the Week/Day

> When … this mortal has put on immortality, then shall be brought to pass the saying that is written: "Death is swallowed up in victory. O Death, where is your sting? O Hades [grave], where is your victory?" … But thanks be to God, who gives us the victory through our Lord Jesus Christ. —1 Corinthians 15:54–57

Devotional 11
Israel's Wilderness Journey with God (Salvation from God Alone)

> The LORD saved Israel that day out of the hand of the Egyptians, and Israel saw the Egyptians dead on the seashore. —Exodus 14:30

> Then Moses and the children of Israel sang this song to the LORD: … "The LORD is my strength and song, and He has become my salvation; He is my God, and I will praise Him." —Exodus 15:1–2

The LORD delivered the children of Israel from the power of the Egyptians. Notice that Moses' name was not mentioned here as saving Israel. Salvation is solely the work of God. He mightily saved Israel—not just partially but completely—that day. The Israelites saw that the Egyptians were dead on the seashore and that all Israel had been delivered. They were so overwhelmed with joy that they burst out with praise and thanksgiving for such a great salvation.

Our Earthly Journey with Jesus (Salvation from God Alone)

> As many as received Him, … He gave the right to become children of God, to those … who were born, not of blood, nor of the will of the flesh, nor of the will of man, but of God. —John 1:12–13

The Father, through Jesus and the power of the Holy Spirit, indwells us (regeneration), gives us new birth (true faith), moves us to have sorrow for sin (repentance), declares sinners to be righteous *in Christ* (justification), restores us to friendship with Him (reconciliation), makes us His children (adoption), increasingly develops holiness in our mortal bodies (sanctification), and completely molds us into the image of Christ (glorification). Salvation is solely the work of God.

What about You?

Salvation means "deliverance from the power of sin." Your salvation is exclusively and completely God's gracious work, not what you have done to earn it. He delivers you from the power of sin the moment you believe (baptism of the Holy Spirit) based on Christ and His work of salvation alone. You will see it by the transformation in yourself; from one who was dead in sin, to one who has experienced salvation *in Christ*. Your response for so great a salvation will be joyful praise and overwhelming adoration. Then by the power of the Holy Spirit, you will want to share it with whomever you meet.

Prayer

Father in heaven, we are thankful that You are in charge of saving those we come in contact with, and are the only one who transforms a person who is dead in sin to salvation *in Christ*. Thank You for using us to bring the message of Your salvation to others and giving us the joy of seeing these persons' lives transformed with our own eyes. Help us not be discouraged when it takes a while for You to work out Your salvation in us and others, but to have patience with Your timing. We give You praise and adoration for what You have done and what You are doing through Jesus and the power of the Holy Spirit. In Jesus' name we pray, amen.

Verse of the Week/Day

> The LORD is my light and my salvation; Whom shall I fear? The LORD is the strength of my life; of whom shall I be afraid? When the wicked came against me to eat up my flesh, my enemies, and foes, they stumbled and fell. Though an army may encamp against me, my heart shall not fear. Though war may rise against me, in this [the LORD's strength and salvation] I will be confident. —Psalm 27:1–3

Devotional 12
Israel's Wilderness Journey with God (Believed by Faith)

> The children of Israel had walked on dry land in the midst of the sea, **and the waters were a wall to them on their right hand and on their left.** … Israel saw the great work which the LORD had done … **so the people feared** and believed **the LORD and His servant Moses.** —Exodus 14:29–31

Can you imagine what it was like to walk between two huge walls of water? Israel saw the power of God and feared (worshipped/believed) the LORD for all He had done against the Egyptians. They also recognized Moses as their God-appointed leader as he led them in their response to God's salvation by faith—walking between the walls of water. They did not believe the LORD blindly, for they had seen all the mighty acts He had performed on their behalf against the Egyptians to bring about their salvation. So, they walked through the midst of the sea completely dependent on God.

God's faithfulness alone was the cause of their trusting Him to bring them through the Red Sea, not on any faith they had mustered up or accomplished themselves.

Our Earthly Journey with Jesus (Believe by Faith)

> "Whosoever believes on Him [Jesus] should not perish, but have eternal life. For God sent not the Son into the world to judge the world; but that the world should be saved through Him." —John 3:16b–17 (ASV)

The phrases *in Him*, *in Jesus*, *in Christ*, and *in God* appear throughout the Bible. To be *in Christ* means that we are children of God walking by His faith and faithfulness alone and not a faith we have achieved. God sees the righteousness of His Son in us and no longer sees our imperfections. Only by the faith/faithfulness of Christ is our sin debt canceled, our relationship with God restored, and eternal life certain. (See Galatians 2:16, 20, and Philippians 3:9 KJV.)

What about You?

To *believe by faith* means "to completely trust in the work God has done through Jesus." True Faith (Jesus) is the foundation of trusting God and is the evidence of spiritual living. True Faith (Jesus) causes you to walk. Because you have been given Jesus Christ, you walked away from this world's ways and sin by faith through the midst of your baptism into your new life *in Christ*. Faith is not blind, for God has shown you in His Word all the mighty acts He has performed on your behalf to bring about your salvation. You, I, and others have been saved through faith, the faith that is *in Christ*. Let me reiterate—not a faith that is of ourselves but the gift from God, the faith of Christ in us. (See Ephesians 2:8 NKJV)

Prayer

Father in heaven, thank You for filling us with the righteousness of Christ. As we respond to Your salvation in our new faith walk *in You*, help us completely trust You because of all the mighty acts You have performed on our behalf. Thank you that *in Jesus*, You have made us Your children and have canceled our debt of sin, restored Your relationship with us, and made our eternity with You certain. You have done marvelous things. Hallelujah to our Lord and Savior, Jesus Christ! In His name we pray, amen.

Verse of the Week/Day

> Let us run with endurance the race that is set before us, looking unto Jesus, the Author and Finisher of faith, who for the joy that was set before Him endured the cross, despising the shame. —Hebrews 12:1–2

Devotional 13
Israel's Wilderness Journey with God (New Life Journey into the Wilderness)
Moses brought Israel from the Red Sea; then they went … into the Wilderness of Shur. —Exodus 15:22a

The *Red* in Red Sea symbolizes blood. The Israelites had just passed through the blood, the water, and the wind in walking by faith on dry ground through the Red Sea. They were at peace with God.

Moses then led them in their new life journey into the wilderness. The Wilderness of Shur was the home of the Ishmaelites and Midianites (both Abraham's sons). It is in modern Arabia according to Galatians 4:25. These two families had been living there for more than four hundred years and no longer believed on the God of Abraham, their father. God brought Israel into the wilderness to sanctify them (to make them holy) and to be a witness (testimony) of God's salvation to those around them. Walking in a wilderness is one-day-at-a-time living. The Israelites would have to depend completely on the LORD—not on themselves—for their spiritual and physical well-being in such a barren, hostile environment.

Our Earthly Journey with Jesus (New Life Journey into the World)
"Sanctify them by Your Truth. Your Word is Truth. As You sent Me [Jesus] into the world, I have sent them into the world. For their sakes I sanctify Myself, that they also may be sanctified." —John 17:17–19

The Truth is Jesus Christ, who was sanctified (set apart) to shed His blood on the cross for us. Jesus is praying for His disciples to be sanctified (made holy) so that they can bring God's message of salvation into this sinful and hostile world. All those who are His and hear the disciples' testimony, with the Holy Spirit's help, will be drawn to Christ for salvation and be made holy.

What about You?
Wilderness means "the sinful world and its value systems." God is bringing you from your new redeemed life *in Christ* into the wilderness of this sinful world, not only for you to be made holy—to live a life of obedience—but also to be a witness, a testimony to a hostile world that needs salvation. Your testimony will also show those who are just beginning their new life *in Christ,* as well as those who have been *in Christ* for many years, what it means to completely depend on Jesus in your (and their) daily walk with Him.

Prayer
Father in heaven, thank You that we do not have to walk in the wilderness of this world alone. Help us to take just one day at a time and not worry about tomorrow. You have sanctified us by the water and justified us by the blood of Christ. May the wind of the Spirit of Truth help us witness to the world and share the gospel with those who need Your salvation. Also, may our testimony guide those who have just started their daily journey (walk) *in You,* and encourage those who have been Christians for many years. In Jesus' name we pray, amen.

Verse of the Week/Day
Who is he [the one] who overcomes the world, but he [the one] who believes that Jesus is the Son of God. This is He who came by water and blood, Jesus Christ; not only by water, but by water and blood. It is the Spirit who bears witness because the Spirit is Truth. There are three that bear witness in Heaven: the Father, the Word, and the Holy Spirit; these three are one. There are three that bear witness on earth: the Spirit [Truth], the Water [Sanctification], and the Blood [Justification]; these three agree as one. —1 John 5:5–8

Devotional 14
Israel's Wilderness Journey with God (Tested on Their Journey)

And they went three days in the wilderness and found no water. Now when they came to Marah, they could not drink the waters, for they were bitter. ... Then the people complained against Moses, saying, "What shall we drink?" —Exodus 15:22b–24

The children of Israel had been traveling along the Red Sea the whole time since leaving Egypt, so water was plentiful. After crossing the Red Sea, they went three days into the wilderness without finding water, so thirst became an issue. They eventually found water, but it was bitter. The first thing they did was complain. Three days earlier, they were praising God at the top of their lungs for all the miraculous works He had performed on their behalf, and dancing with all their might for His having saved them from their enemy.

This was God's first test for them. He allowed them to become thirsty to see if they remembered that they needed to depend on Him and call on Him to remedy this situation. This is what Psalm 106:11–13 says: "The waters covered their enemies so there was not one of them left. Then they believed the LORD's words and sang His praise, but they soon forgot His works; they did not wait for His counsel." The people never asked God for help. Instead, they blamed Moses.

Our Earthly Journey with Jesus (Tested on Our Journey)

Jesus lifted up His eyes, and seeing a great multitude coming toward Him, He said to Philip, "Where shall we buy bread, that these may eat?" But this He said to test him, for He Himself knew what He would do. Philip answered Him, "Two hundred denarii worth of bread is not sufficient for them, that every one of them may have a little." One of His disciples, Andrew, Simon Peter's brother, said to Him, "There is a lad here who has five barley loaves and two small fish, but what are they among so many?" —John 6:5–9

Jesus had already performed miracles in the disciples' presence, but they forgot He had the power to remedy this situation. He was testing the disciples and waiting for: (my words) "Lord, we believe you can feed these people. Work in and through us to accomplish Your will." If we were confronted by Jesus in that situation, would we have failed the test too?

What about You?

Tested means "to examine closely." Is God testing you? Do you have days where things are not going well, or you make plans without including Him? Are you complaining about others or are others complaining about you? All through your walk in this world, you will be confronted by problems. Will you turn to yourself or others first for help, or will you go to God in prayer asking for His guidance? God will examine you closely. Will you pass the test?

Prayer

Father in heaven, as we confront a sinful world, guide us in our walk with You on this wilderness journey. We confess that we tend to look at things from a physical perspective first before we see things from a spiritual perspective. Test us and help us to depend on You in everything and not ourselves or others. Thank You for Your daily provisions. In Jesus' name we pray, amen.

Verse of the Week/Day

Search me, O God, and know my heart; try [test] me, and know my anxieties. —Psalm 139:23

Devotional 15
Israel's Wilderness Journey with God (God Used a Tree to Draw Israel to Himself)
> So, Moses cried out to the LORD, and the LORD showed him a tree. When he cast it into the waters, the waters were made sweet. —Exodus 15:25a

The word *show* means "instructing or directing/pointing out." God began instructing, guiding, and directing the Israelites in their walk on this new journey. Though they failed the first test, God in His mercy forgave them and showed (pointed out to) Moses a tree to make the water sweet. The bitter water symbolized the bitterness of their lives and showed them their unbelief and sin. God drew them to drink by sweetening that bitter water with the tree so they could freely experience/drink His love, mercy, and forgiveness as He led them on this new journey from bondage of Egypt to His freedom in Canaan.

Our Earthly Journey with Jesus (God Uses a Tree/Cross to Draw Us to Jesus)
> [Jesus said], "My soul is troubled, and what shall I say? 'Father, save Me from this hour'? But for this purpose I came to this hour. Father, glorify Your Name." Then a voice came from heaven, saying, "I have both glorified it and will glorify it again." … Jesus … said, "This voice did not come because of Me, but for your sake. Now is the judgment of this world; now the ruler of this world will be cast out. And I, if I am lifted up from the earth, will draw all peoples [nations] to Myself." —John 12:27–33

The Father glorified His name by pointing out our remedy for sin, Jesus, who as God/man perfectly passed the test. God cast the sin that was in us on Jesus, who took on Himself our bitterness—sin, on another tree—the cross. Because He suffered the bitterness of our sins by His death on the cross, Jesus drew us and all nations—not just the Israelites—to Himself. He drew us to freely drink the sweetness of new life by showing us mercy, forgiving our sins, and making us right with God for all eternity.

What about You?
To *draw* means "to move by love." God is moved by His love for you and draws/moves you to love Him. When you cry out to the Lord, He hears you by showing you His love through Jesus' sacrifice on the cross. The purpose of Christ's death on the cross was to pay for your sins so you could freely drink His love and mercy. By the tree (cross), all those who are drawn by love to Him are shown grace and mercy and are forgiven. They end their old life of sin and are given a new life devoted to Jesus.

Prayer
Father in heaven, though we fail so often in our walk with You, dealing daily with the bitterness of sin in our lives and complaining about the circumstances we find ourselves in, You still draw us back with Your grace, love, and mercy through the cross of Jesus. May we show that same love and mercy to a world that needs to be drawn to You for salvation and to others who are already *in Christ* and need to be drawn closer and closer to You by Your Word of instruction, freely letting them drink the Water of Life—Jesus. Thank You for quenching our thirst through the power of Your Holy Spirit. In Jesus' name we pray, amen.

Verse of the Week/Day
> The Spirit and the bride say, "Come!" And let him [anyone] who hears say, "Come!" And let him [anyone] who thirsts come. Whoever desires, let him [them] take the water of life freely. —Revelation 22:17

Devotional 16
Israel's Wilderness Journey with God (Faith Walk Based on Obedience—God Alone Heals)

> There He tested them, and said, "If you diligently heed [obey] the voice of the LORD your God and do what is right in His sight, give ear to His commandments and keep all His statutes, I will put none of the diseases on you which I have brought on the Egyptians. For I am the LORD who heals you." —Exodus 15:25b–26

Yahweh Rapha means "Jesus, your Healer." The bitter water had been healed by God with a tree. Yahweh (Jesus) had begun the process of testing them to see if they would walk by faith and depend on Him for obedience/healing. He wanted them to be holy, but that could only happen if they acknowledged that He alone was their healer. It was Yahweh's holiness/healing, not Israel's righteousness/works, that would help them respond with obedience to His commands/will. Notice I said process, because learning obedience/submission to God's will was going to require their entire wilderness journey with God to complete.

Our Earthly Journey with Jesus (Faith Walk Based on Obedience—Jesus Alone Heals)

> A certain man … had an infirmity thirty-eight years. When Jesus saw him lying there, … He said to him, "Do you want to be made well?" The sick man answered Him, "Sir, I have no man to put me into the pool when the water is stirred up; but while I am coming, another steps down before me." Jesus said to him, "Rise, take up your bed and walk." And immediately the man was made well, took up his bed, and walked. … The man … told the Jews that it was Jesus who had made him well. —John 5:5–15

Jerusalem had a pool where a great number of sick people resided. The Bible says that the pool was stirred once a year by an angel and that whoever went into the pool first after the stirring would be healed of his or her disease. There was a man who had been sick for thirty-eight years hoping to be healed, but he had never been able to get to the pool. He had spent most of his life trying on his own to get well. When Jesus—Yahweh Rapha—came to this place, He healed the man both spiritually and physically before he could respond with obedience. At Jesus' command, he was immediately made well. Able then to obey Jesus' Word, he got up and walked. Later, he acknowledged that it was Jesus, not himself, who was his Healer.

What about You?
Obedience means "submitting to someone else's will." For the Christian, it is submitting to God's will. Non-Christians will not submit to God's will, nor can they do so (see Romans 8:6–8). Jesus' death on the cross accomplished our healing, helping us to respond with obedience and submission to His Word/Will. Remember that your faith walk is based on the holiness and obedience of Christ, who resides in you, not your own righteousness. To put it simply: *Holiness is Jesus in you, fulfilling (obeying) the will of the Father through you.* Submitting obediently to God's will is a lifelong process. So, do not be discouraged.

Prayer
Father in heaven, when you created us, you made us holy, but sin took that holiness away and made us spiritually sick/dead. Thank You for healing us through Christ's obedient death on the cross so we could live again, filled with His righteousness and obedience. Help us and those we interact with to submit to and obey Your Word, that daily, not our will but only Your will be done in and through us. In Jesus' name we pray, amen.

Verse of the Week/Day

> [Jesus] Himself, bore our sins in His own body on the tree [cross], that we, having died to sins, might live for righteousness; by whose stripes you were healed. —1 Peter 2:24

Devotional 17
Israel's Wilderness Journey with God (A Brief Rest on the Journey)
> Then they came to Elim, where there were twelve wells [fountains] of water and seventy palm trees; so they camped there by the waters. —Exodus 15:27

It must have been a welcome relief when the Israelites came to this place. They had been traveling in a desert since they had left Egypt. This was the first time they could enjoy rest at an oasis, which had twelve fountains (possibly one for each tribe) and seventy palm trees (possibly one for each family unit). This was the perfect setting for them to reflect on all God had done for them on their journey with Him thus far and to prepare for the rest of the journey. (A table in the back of this book shows the twelve tribes and seventy family units of Israel.)

Our Earthly Journey with Jesus (A Brief Rest on Our Journey)
> He [Jesus] went down to Capernaum; He, His mother, His brothers, and His disciples; and they did not stay there many days. —John 2:12

> Jesus, therefore, being wearied from His journey, sat thus, [rested] by the well. … A woman of Samaria came to draw water. Jesus said to her, "Give Me a drink." … Then the woman of Samaria said to Him, "How is it that You, being a Jew, ask a drink from me, a Samaritan woman?" … Jesus answered and said to her, "If you knew … who it is who says to you, 'Give Me a drink,' you would have asked Him, and He would have given you living water." —John 4:6–10

Occasionally, Jesus stopped to rest briefly with His family and friends at their home in Capernaum to catch up on each other's activities. On another occasion, Jesus spent a couple of days with the people of Sychar, resting physically in the middle of a long trip on foot from Jerusalem to Galilee. While resting from physical weariness, He gave the people of Sychar spiritual drink, a drink of Himself, the Living Water, rest for their souls that would last for the remainder of their lives and into eternity.

What about You?
Rest means "to have relief; peace of mind and spirit." On this arid journey through life, you and I often think of rest as something for our own benefit or laziness. But God wants rest to be more than that. You come to an oasis when you share with your family and loved ones what God has been doing in your life since you last met. You also come to an oasis through your ministry concerning those who do not have salvation and share with them a drink of Jesus, the Living Water, which gives them spiritual relief from the cares of this world—rest for their souls for the remainder of their lives on earth and into eternity. You have peace of mind and spirit when you rest in the fountains of salvation and the palm tree blessings God has given you.

Prayer
Father in heaven, thank You for the oases in our lives on this arid journey and for giving us time to rest in the fountains of salvation and the palm tree blessings You have given us on our earthly journey with You. Help us in our rest to share with our family and friends what You have been doing in our lives. Further, help us to share with the world Your great love and salvation in store for them through Jesus Christ, giving them rest for their souls now and into eternity. In Jesus' name we pray, amen.

Verse of the Week/Day
> "Come to Me, all you who labor and are heavy laden, and I [Jesus] will give you rest." —Matthew 11:28

Devotional 18
Israel's Wilderness Journey with God (Manna—Bread from Heaven)
> The LORD said to Moses, "Behold, I will rain bread from heaven for you. And the people shall go out and gather a certain quota every day, that I may test them, whether they will walk in My law or not." —Exodus 16:4

The food supply from Egypt was gone. God again tested the Israelites dependence on Him by allowing them to hunger, to see if they would ask Him to supply food for them without complaining first and trust Him alone to faithfully provide for each day. Instead they complained once more, quickly forgetting all that God had done thus far in their walk with Him to meet all their needs. Yet He showed them mercy and miraculously rained down manna from heaven, food that would sustain them for the rest of the journey to Canaan. Every morning when the dew appeared, so would the bread. When the Israelites first saw the manna, they asked, "What is it?," which is what the word *manna* means. So Moses told them it was the bread God had said He would provide daily to satisfy their physical hunger.

Our Earthly Journey with Jesus (Jesus—Bread from Heaven)
> Jesus said to them, "Most assuredly, I say to you, Moses did not give you the bread from heaven, but My Father gives you the True Bread from heaven. For the Bread of God is He who comes down from heaven and gives life to the world." —John 6:32–33

Jesus had just finished telling the people to depend on Him for spiritual as well as physical food, but they misunderstood Him and asked Him what they should do to accomplish the works of God and take care of all those needs. Jesus told them they could not do His works or provide for their needs. Just as manna (physical food) was provided by God in the wilderness and not by Moses, so too, they needed to depend on God to provide their spiritual food. It was the Father's work alone to send Jesus—the true Bread from heaven—to give life to the world; not just physical food (recall that by the Word of God spoken at creation in Genesis chapter one; physical foods—grasses, herbal plants, and fruit trees—were provided on day three), but also spiritual food, the Word of God (Jesus), who/which is necessary for eternal life.

What about You?
Bread means "life-giving food." In this world, you need to depend on God—Father, Son, and Holy Spirit—to meet your physical and spiritual needs. All food comes from God—physical food to sustain your body and spiritual food to sustain your soul. Only by Jesus Christ, the Word of God—your spiritual food (Bread from heaven)—can you believe, obey, eat, and live.

Prayer
Father in heaven, sustain us physically and spiritually. Help us emphasize the latter—the spiritual, knowing that you will also provide the former—the physical. Thank you for Jesus, the true Bread from heaven. By the Holy Spirit's power, help us depend on You alone to give us and those who receive You, the faith that is *in Christ* to believe, obey, eat, and live. In Jesus' name we pray, amen.

Verse of the Week/Day
> … "The LORD your God led you all the way these forty years in the wilderness, to humble you and test you, to know what was in your heart, whether you would keep His commandments or not. So He … allowed you to hunger … that He might make you know that man shall not live by [physical] bread alone; but … by every word that proceeds from the mouth of the LORD." —Deuteronomy 8:2–3

Devotional 19
Israel's Wilderness Journey with God (God's Manna Came Daily—Test of Faith)

> Moses said, "Let no one leave any of it [the manna] till morning." … They did not heed [obey] Moses, but some of them left part of it until morning, and it bred worms and stank. And Moses was angry with them. So they gathered it every morning, every man according to his need. —Exodus 16:19–21a

In our last devotional, we learned that God gave the Israelites manna daily. He commanded the people to gather each morning just enough manna to satisfy the need of every person in their household. But some disobeyed and saved part of the manna for the next day and it spoiled. Through Moses, God was teaching the people to trust and obey Him, to depend on Him for each days' needs only, not the next day and beyond.

There was one exception. God required them to rest on the Sabbath/seventh day. So, He told Moses to have the people gather enough manna on the sixth day for both that day and the Sabbath. Again, some disobeyed and went hungry on the Sabbath.

Our Earthly Journey with Jesus (Jesus Is Our *Daily Bread*—Test of Faith)

> Then they said to Him, "Lord, give us this bread always." And Jesus said to them, "I am the Bread of Life. He [anyone] who comes to Me shall never hunger, and he [anyone] who believes in [on (KJV)] Me shall never thirst. But I said … you have seen Me and yet do not believe." —John 6:34–36

This issue seems to come up repeatedly with Jesus' followers. They asked Jesus to give them their physical bread every day from then on, but again, Jesus was not talking about physical bread, but spiritual bread which gives eternal life. The eternal food He was giving would keep them from hungering and thirsting again spiritually, but the people did not understand because all they were concerned about was their physical needs, things they could see, touch, and feel—things that were temporal. They did not believe or trust Him even though they witnessed His miracles.

What about You?
Daily means "repeats on a day to day basis." Do you seem to be overconcerned about physical needs, having enough for today, tomorrow; this week, next week; this year, next year? Jesus taught us to pray, "Give us this day our daily bread" (Matthew 6:11 NKJV). Do you believe that God is the One who not only wants to but is able to give you daily all you need for your body and soul? Do you fret about tomorrow? He will give you tomorrow what you need tomorrow. God wants you to completely depend on Him one day at a time, and trust Him to meet your body's and soul's needs daily on this wilderness journey with Jesus in this world. Wilderness living is one-day-at-a-time living; no more, no less.

Prayer
Father in heaven, we know that this subject comes up frequently in our daily walk with You because we think we are in control of our physical needs, and You our spiritual needs, but You are in control of both. Keep us from fretting about the future. Help us seek Your righteousness first and depend on You for only today's needs concerning body and soul, leaving tomorrow's needs in Your hands as we walk on this wilderness journey, with You sustaining us. In Jesus' name we pray, amen.

Verse of the Week/Day

> "What shall we eat? … What shall we drink? … Seek first the kingdom of God and His righteousness, and all these things shall be added to you. Therefore, do not worry about tomorrow." —Matthew 6:31–34

Devotional 20
Israel's Wilderness Journey with God (Manna—Gather before the Heat of the Day)
> They gathered it [manna] every morning, every man according to his [family's] need. And when the sun became hot, it melted. —Exodus 16:21

When God spoke, a response of obedience was needed from Israel, which required gathering manna early in the morning before the manna melted. This verse implies that if a household did not gather manna by the time the sun burned off the morning dew, there would be no food for them that day. That family would go hungry and unprepared for the day's activities. Once more, God was testing the Israelites to see if they would trust and obey all His commands.

Our Earthly Journey with Jesus (Prayer—Food before the *Heat of the Day*)
> Then Simon Peter, having a sword, drew it and struck the high priest's servant, and cut off his right ear.
> —John 18:10

> … They said to him, "You are not also one of His disciples, are you?" He denied it and said, "I am not!" One of the servants of the high priest, a relative of him whose ear Peter cut off, said, "Did I not see you in the garden with Him?" Peter then denied again; and immediately a rooster crowed. —John 18:25–27

In New Testament times, the day started when the rooster crowed—just before sunrise. Here, we read that Peter cut off the right ear of the high priest's servant and denied that he knew Jesus all before the rooster crowed. Earlier that morning on the Mount of Olives (according to Luke 22:45 NIV), Jesus had asked Peter, "Why are you sleeping? Get up and pray so that you will not fall into temptation." Because he did not listen to Jesus and pray before the *heat of the day*, he was spiritually starved and fell into temptation, using a sword to protect Jesus from the mob who had come to arrest Him, and denying that he knew Jesus because he was afraid of being arrested himself.

What about You?
Heat of the day means "time of day when activities, pressures, and concerns intensify." Do you start your day with the Lord in His Word and prayer, or do you skip the spiritual food and go into the *heat of the day* unprepared? When the activities and pressures of the day intensify, you will not be able to stand against temptation but will melt—yield to it. Have you asked God to help you set aside time so you can begin each day with spiritual food—the Word of God and prayer, the sword and shield that equip you for victory against temptation and evil? The Holy Spirit will protect you and keep you from yielding to temptation.

Prayer
Father in heaven, thank You that we do not have to face the day alone and that You have a remedy to support us. Through the obedience of Christ in us, help us spend time each day with You in prayer, reading Your Word, and meditating upon it; not mindless meditating like the world, but minds filled with the thoughts/knowledge of Christ. Equip us with Your sword and shield against the evil one so that before the *heat of the day*—when things intensify and become hectic, we may be able to obey Your will. With the Holy Spirit's power, help us stand against temptation and not yield to it. In Jesus' name we pray, amen.

Verse of the Week/Day
> Consider my meditation. Give heed to the voice of my cry, my King, and my God, for to You I will pray. My voice You shall hear in the morning, O LORD; in the morning I will direct it to You, and I will look up. —Psalm 5:1b–3

Devotional 21
Israel's Wilderness Journey with God (Rephidim—Struggle Against/Tempting God)

> There was no water for the people to drink. Therefore, the people contended with Moses, and said, "Give us water, that we may drink." So, Moses said to them, "Why do you contend [struggle] with me? Why do you tempt the LORD?" … Moses cried out to the LORD, saying, "What shall I do with this people? They are almost ready to stone me!" —Exodus 17:1–4

Rephidim, on the plain at the foot of Mount Sinai, was where the children of Israel complained again about having no water. They did not go to the LORD first but again blamed Moses, even after all God had done to deliver them from slavery and bring them thus far on their journey with Him. Moses was only an instrument of God—the go-between or intercessor, not the source for satisfying their needs. Through their complaining, they were sinfully asking God to prove Himself again and again. Their old sinful nature was fighting the new spiritual life they had received *in Yahweh/Jesus.*

Our Earthly Journey with Jesus (No Trust—Struggle Against/Tempting Jesus)

> The Jews … said to Him, "How long do you keep us in doubt? If you are the Christ, tell us plainly." Jesus answered, "I told you, and you do not believe." … Then the Jews took up stones again to stone him. Jesus answered them, "Many good works I have shown you from My Father. For which of those works do you stone Me?" The Jews answered Him, saying, … "For blasphemy, and because You, being a Man, make Yourself God."
> —John 10:24–33

The Jews still did not comprehend who Jesus really was. He was not the type of Messiah they were looking for. They were looking for a King and Savior who would set them free from Rome. Jesus had not come to take over the nation of Israel and fight Rome; He came to be God's suffering instrument, the Savior who would fight against and die for their sin and the sin of the world. The Pharisees struggled against Jesus' claim to be God, so they picked up stones to stone Him. In their sin of unbelief, they pressed Jesus to prove He was the Messiah.

What about You?

To *tempt* God means "to prove His authority and faithfulness." Are you unbelieving? Do you have this constant war in your life? Spiritually, you know God will meet all your needs as He promised because He has been faithful in all His works concerning you. But in your flesh—your old sinful nature—you struggle against God by doubting His faithfulness and tempt (test) Him to prove Himself as God. Ask Jesus to deliver you from this sinful struggle, and patiently wait for Him to supply all your daily needs.

Prayer

Father in heaven, forgive us! Through the faith of Jesus Christ in us, help us always put our trust in You and not struggle against You—asking You to prove Yourself as God, but to submit to Your will. Deliver us daily, with the Holy Spirit's power, from our evil ways of tempting You and doubting Your faithfulness in our lives. In Jesus' name we pray, amen.

Verse of the Week/Day

> I [Paul] delight in the law of God according to the inward [spiritual] man. But I see another law in my [physical] members, warring against the law of my mind. … O wretched man that I am! Who will deliver me? … Thank God—through Jesus Christ our Lord! —Romans 7:22–25

Devotional 22
Israel's Wilderness Journey with God (Water from the Rock Quenches Thirst)

> And the LORD said to Moses, "Go on before the people, and take with you some of the elders of Israel. Also take in your hand your rod with which you struck the river, and go. Behold, I will stand before you there on the rock in Horeb; and you shall strike the rock, and water will come out of it, that the people may drink."
>
> —Exodus 17:5–6a

Moses was told to go part of the way up the mountain to the rock of Horeb with two things, the rod of God and the elders of Israel. The rod represented God's authority and discipline, His will, and it was to be used to strike the rock. The seventy elders represented the seventy family units of Israel. The rock represented Yahweh (Jesus Christ), who would stand before them on the rock. God wanted to show them who He was, and despite their unworthiness, to display His mercy again. When they came to the rock, Moses was commanded to strike it with the rod and water would gush out to quench the people's thirst.

Our Earthly Journey with Jesus (Water from *the Rock* Quenches Thirst)

> Jesus answered, … "If you knew the gift of God, and who it is who says to you, 'Give Me a drink,' you would have asked Him, and He would have given you living water." … The woman said to Him, "I know that Messiah is coming." … Jesus said, "I who speak to you am He." —John 4:10–26

While Jesus was resting from a long journey from Jerusalem to Galilee and the disciples had gone into the city to buy food, a woman came to the well where He was sitting. Jesus told her that He had living water that would keep her from thirsting again. The woman thought Jesus was talking about quenching physical thirst, but when Jesus told her about everything that had happened in her life and that He was the Messiah she was looking for, she was transformed from living a life of sin to overflowing with the living (spiritual) water He promised. Jesus was showing her grace and mercy despite her unworthiness.

What about You?

Rock means "protection, faithfulness, and trustworthiness." In the last devotional, we discussed struggling with God and testing His authority, protection, faithfulness, and trustworthiness. Despite your unworthiness, He displays His grace and mercy to you through His protective, faithful, never-changing love. Jesus is *the Rock*, the Living Water you can drink from and live.

You have *the Rock* in you, the Fountain that quenches your spiritual thirst and overflows back to God in praise and thanksgiving; and also to others, so you can show those you encounter His grace and mercy despite their sin and unworthiness.

Prayer

Father in heaven, thank You for flooding us with Your protective, faithful, never-changing love, and showing us Your grace and mercy despite our unworthiness and unbelief. May the love of *the Rock* of our salvation overflow from us back to You for so great a salvation; and also to others, so their thirst may be quenched by the Living Water, Jesus Christ. May that same grace and mercy, through the power of the Holy Spirit, cause their lives to be transformed from sinfulness to the holiness and righteousness of Christ. In His name we pray, amen.

Verse of the Week/Day

> [All Israel] drank the same spiritual drink, for they drank of the *spiritual Rock* that accompanied them, and *that Rock was Christ.* —1 Corinthians 10:4 (NIV); emphasis added

Devotional 23
Israel's Wilderness Journey with God (Elders Witnessed Striking the Rock)

> "Behold, I [the LORD] will stand before you there on the rock in Horeb; and you shall strike the rock, and water will come out of it, that the people may drink." Moses did so in the sight of the elders of Israel. So he called the name of the place Massah and Meribah, because of the contention of the children of Israel, and because they tempted the LORD, saying, "Is the LORD among us or not?" —Exodus 17:6–7

Moses brought the rod symbolizing God's authority and discipline, and the seventy elders of Israel, the people's representatives, to witness publicly the striking of the rock representing Yahweh/Jesus, the power and faithfulness of God. Instead of punishing Israel for its struggle against Moses and Himself, God told Moses to strike the rock, Yahweh/Jesus. The Bible says that when the rock was struck, it split and water came gushing out, more than enough to satisfy all Israel. The water continued flowing from the rock to quench the thirst of Israel the whole year they were at Mount Sinai.

Our Earthly Journey with Jesus (Sanhedrin Witnessed Striking *the Rock*)

> The soldiers twisted a crown of thorns and put it on His head, and they put on Him a purple robe. Then they said, "Hail, King of the Jews!" And they struck Him with their hands. —John 19:2–3

The Sanhedrin included seventy elders and the high priest, the same as the Old Testament. As the soldiers and others struck and beat Jesus publicly, they (the elders) watched with hatred in their hearts. Yet because Jesus loved us, He endured the torment from humanity humbly, and suffered the wrath of God for our sin on the cross, giving His life to pay the sin penalty—death. He gave Himself in obedience to God so we might have the continuous Living Water instead of death—separation from God—which we all deserved.

What about You?

To *strike* means "to brutally beat, torment." The Bible says we all strayed away from God going our own way of sin. We too are guilty of looking with distain on Jesus. Because we have all sinned, you and I too, so to speak, watched as Jesus, *the Rock*, was beaten. He took on Himself our sins and the torment we deserved. He loved you and me so much that He willingly suffered every blow of the rod, every slap on His body, every spit in His face, every strike of the jagged whip on His back, every thorn that pierced His brow, every nail that was hammered through His hands and feet, and every insult directed at His holy name, for our sake.

Prayer

Lord Jesus, thank You for taking the beating and torment we deserved. Help us understand the enormity and horror of Your suffering on the way to the cross and on the cross. Forgive us as we watched with distain and then hid our faces from You, taking lightly the punishment You bore for our sins. Your love for us is so amazing and so needed! Forgive us! In Your name we pray, amen.

Verse of the Week/Day

> He was despised and rejected by men [us, the human race], a Man of sorrows and acquainted with grief. And we hid, as it were, our faces from Him; He was despised, and we did not esteem Him. Surely He has borne our griefs and carried our sorrows; yet we esteemed Him stricken, smitten by [struck by the rod of] God, and afflicted.
> —Isaiah 53:3–4

Devotional 24
Israel's Wilderness Journey with God (Enemy Attacked When Least Expected)
Now Amalek came and fought with Israel in Rephidim. —Exodus 17:8

Amalek was from the family of Esau, a fierce and nomadic people who often attacked other people indiscriminately. They were the first enemy Israel had to face in the wilderness on their way to Canaan. Without warning, the Amalekites attacked the unprepared Israelites. So God told Moses He would erase Amalek's descendants from the face of the earth. That came to pass during the time of Esther, when Haman, Amalek's descendant, tried to destroy the Jewish nation. Instead, Haman was hanged, and the Jews destroyed the Amalekites, fulfilling God's prophecy.

Our Earthly Journey with Jesus (Enemy Attacks When Least Expected)
He [Jesus] was troubled in spirit, and testified and said, "Most assuredly, I say to you, one of you will betray Me." … He [John] said to Him, "Lord, who is it?" Jesus answered, "It is he to whom I shall give a piece of bread when I have dipped it." And having dipped the bread, He gave it to Judas Iscariot, the son of Simon. Now after the piece of bread, Satan entered him. —John 13:21–27

The night before Jesus' suffering and death, while He and His disciples were celebrating their last Passover together and enjoying each other's company, Satan entered Judas Iscariot to betray Jesus. Jesus knew what was happening with Judas, but the other disciples were caught off guard.

Satan was the first enemy of Adam and Eve and everyone who has lived. But God sent Jesus—the Word of God—to defeat Satan the next day by dying on the cross and three days later rising from the dead. Jesus will completely destroy Satan and all his host when He comes back at the end of time.

What about You?
Enemy means "spiritual adversary." An adversary is one who attacks. So often your enemy, Satan, the devil, attacks you when you least expect it. He will attack you through the lure of worldly attractions and through evil disguised as good. Sometimes he attacks you in your own flesh or through others including those you know and love. The cruelty of Satan, who seeks to devour you any way he can, is overcome by watchfulness and faith. You cannot stand up to Satan alone. Only with the Word of God in you and the armor of God on you can he be defeated. One thing to remember is that Satan does not have free reign over earth, but is under the sovereign, watchful eye of God concerning you, His child. Someday, He will be destroyed, completely erased from the face of the earth.

Prayer
Father in heaven; the devil seeks to devour us, the world disguises evil as good, and our flesh is tempted by its enticements daily. Put Your armor on us so we can withstand the devil's attacks. By faith and through the power of the Holy Spirit, help us watch and pray until You have destroyed the devil's work and every foe against You. In Jesus' name we pray, amen.

Verse of the Week/Day
Be sober, be vigilant [watchful]; because your adversary the devil walks about like a roaring lion, seeking whom he may devour. Resist him, [standing] steadfast in the faith, knowing that the same sufferings are experienced by your brotherhood [brothers and sisters *in Christ*] in the world. —1 Peter 5:8–9

Devotional 25
Israel's Wilderness Journey with God (Moses Depending on the Flesh)

> Moses said to Joshua, "Choose us some men and go out, fight with Amalek. Tomorrow I will stand on the top of the hill with the rod of God in my hand." So Joshua did as Moses said to him. … When Moses held up his hand, … Israel prevailed; and when he let down his hand, Amalek prevailed. But Moses' hands became heavy.
> —Exodus 17:9–12a

Lifted hands was the posture of prayer. Moses was praying to God as well as holding up the rod. This passage implies that Moses might have thought he was able to hold the Rod of God by himself while praying; for when his hands were up, the Israelites prevailed, but when his hands were down, the Amalekites prevailed. Prayer can be hard, especially when done with intensity and over an extended period of time, not to mention, holding a staff at the same time. Eventually, Moses' strength failed, and he needed help.

Our Earthly Journey with Jesus (Depending on Our Own Strength)

> The sea arose because a great wind was blowing. So when they had rowed about three or four miles, they saw Jesus walking on the sea and drawing near the boat; and they were afraid. But He said to them, "It is I; do not be afraid." Then they willingly received Him into the boat, and immediately, the boat was at the land where they were going. —John 6:18–21

Jesus had left by Himself to go to a mountain to pray. Meanwhile, the disciples got into their boat, and by themselves, made their way toward Capernaum. Shortly into their trip, a storm came up and a powerful wind overtook them. It takes work to row a boat when the water is calm, but can you imagine rowing a boat when the wind is blowing? And for three to four miles? Their strength was gone, and they needed help. But then Jesus showed up, and when they received Him in the boat, they were immediately at their destination.

What about You?
Flesh means "human strength." There is a story about a man on a plane who refused to fasten his seatbelt because he claimed to be superman; so the stewardess asked him why he needed a jet to fly. How many times have you tried to do things on your own before you turned to Jesus for help? Human strength can go only so far. On your own, you are weak, helpless. Only with Jesus, through the power of the Holy Spirit, can you flourish and live.

Prayer
Father in heaven, we confess that by our own strength, which eventually dries up like a shrub in the desert, we are weak and hopeless. We acknowledge that sometimes we are stubborn and try to do things on our own. Keep us from running ahead of You and putting our trust in ourselves. Help us always turn to You first and put our hope and trust in You alone, so like a tree by the water we will flourish and live. Thank You for Jesus and the power of the Holy Spirit in us. In Jesus' name we pray, amen.

Verse of the Week/Day

> Cursed is the man [one] who trusts in man and makes flesh his strength, whose heart departs from the LORD, for he [they] shall be like a shrub in the desert. … Blessed is the man [one] who trusts in the LORD, whose hope is the LORD. For he [they] shall be like a tree planted by the waters. —Jeremiah 17:5–8a

Devotional 26
Israel's Wilderness Journey with God (Moses' Brothers Help Him)
> Moses' hands became heavy; so they took a stone and put it under him, and he sat on it. Then Aaron and Hur supported his hands, one on one side, and the other on the other side; and his hands were steady until the going down of the sun. —Exodus 17:12

Aaron was Moses' older brother, and Hur was believed to be Moses' brother-in-law, Miriam's husband. While Joshua fought the Amalekites, Moses held his hands up in prayer while holding the staff of God. But his arms grew tired, so Aaron and Hur sat him on a rock, and standing on each side of Moses, held his arms up until the battle was won. That act of working together showed their obedience to God and support for one another. God honored that and brought the victory to the Israelites working through Moses, Aaron, Hur, and Joshua.

Servanthood started with the leadership, an example to the people of how they were to serve one another. This was beneficial for all and brought them together as a community, working for the good of others.

Our Earthly Journey with Jesus (Helping Our Brothers and Sisters)
> So when He [Jesus] had washed their feet, taken His garments, and sat down again, He said to them [the disciples], … "I have given you an example, that you should do as I have done to you. Most assuredly, I say to you, a servant is not greater than his master; nor is he who is sent greater than he who sent him. If you know these things, blessed are you if you do [obey] them [God's command to serve one another]." —John 13:12–17

Jesus, their Master, Teacher, and Rabbi had just washed the feet of His disciples as an example of how they were to serve one another. In those days, if you were a rabbi, you were at the top of the hierarchy, and all those who followed you were your servants and fulfilled your every wish. But Jesus turned that tradition on its head and set an example of servanthood, though His position was higher than those of His disciples. They soon would be the leadership, and He wanted them to work as a body of believers who served one another so His church would flourish.

What about You?
Help means "one who gives support, a servant." God is calling you to serve for the good of others. You are to serve side by side, supporting one another in prayer, struggles, encouragement, and celebrating victories won in the name of Jesus. When that happens, all needs are met and the church flourishes. Leaders need to be examples of what servanthood and loving-kindness look like. This includes parents with their children, employers with their employees, church leaders with their parishioners, and so on.

Prayer
Father in heaven, thank You for Jesus' example of how we are to be servants of all whether or not our position is higher than another's. Help us serve side by side, humbly supporting one another in prayer, struggles, encouragement, and victories won in the name of Jesus without selfish motives. In Jesus' name we pray, amen.

Verse of the Week/Day
> Let nothing be done through selfish ambition or conceit, but in lowliness of mind let each esteem others better than himself [yourself]. —Philippians 2:3

Devotional 27
Israel's Wilderness Journey with God (Aaron: Priest/Intercessor—Hur: Noble/Blameless)
> Moses' hands became heavy; so they took a stone and put it under him, and he sat on it. Aaron and Hur supported his hands, one on one side, and the other on the other side; and his hands were steady until the going down of the sun. So Joshua defeated Amalek and his people with the edge of the sword. … Moses built an altar and called its name, The-LORD-Is-My-Banner. —Exodus 17:12–15

In the Bible, names have meanings, and this passage is no exception. The name *Aaron* means "enlightened one." He was the intercessor between Moses and Pharaoh. Later, he became the high priest, the intercessor between Israel and God. The name *Hur* means "noble, blameless." The significance of their supporting Moses in prayer was this: Moses, who was praying and holding up the rod of Yahweh, (the LORD's saving power), needed the help of Hur (blameless) and Aaron (intercessor) to bring Israel victory over Amalek. By the power of the LORD, their banner, and the servanthood and obedience of all the leadership, God gave the victory to the Israelites over Amalek. (In Hebrew, Yahweh Nissi means "The LORD Is My Banner—the LORD's saving power.")

Our Earthly Journey with Jesus (Jesus: Priest/Intercessor—Jesus: Righteous/Blameless)
> "I [Jesus] have given them Your Word; the world has hated them because they are not of the world, just as I am not of the world. I do not pray that You [Father] should take them out of the world, but that You should keep them from the evil one. They are not of the world, just as I am not of the world." —John 17:14–16

God's Word caused Jesus' disciples to be hated by the world. Thus Jesus—the LORD's saving power; the perfect, righteous High Priest, the blameless Intercessor—was praying for His disciples. He prayed that as they journeyed through this sinful world, though they were no longer of it, would be victorious over their enemies—the devil, sin, and death—through the Holy Spirit's power.

What about You?
Righteous Priest means "blameless intercessor" or "go-between." Everything that Moses, Aaron, and Hur represented together, Jesus is. Jesus is your righteous Priest, the one who sacrificed His own life by shedding His blood on the cross to take away the guilt of your sins, and brought about your justification and righteousness. Jesus is your blameless Intercessor, your go-between, the one who prays to the Father for you. Jesus is your Banner, the one who powerfully gives you victory over your enemies—the devil, sin, and death. By the Holy Spirit's indwelling, you are one *in Christ* and an heir of heaven.

Prayer
Father in heaven, thank You for Jesus, our powerful Banner, who saved us from the evil one and death, who blotted out forever the remembrance of our sins, who made us righteous in Your eyes, and who is always interceding for us. Through Jesus, we are one *in You* and heirs of heaven. In Jesus' name, our righteous Priest, blameless Intercessor, and saving Power we pray, amen.

Verse of the Week/Day
> Therefore, He [Jesus] is also able to save to the uttermost those who come to God through Him, since He always lives to make intercession for them. For such a High Priest was fitting for us, who is holy, harmless, undefiled, separate from sinners, and has become higher than the heavens. —Hebrews 7:25–26

Devotional 28
Israel's Wilderness Journey with God (Jethro Drawn to God through Witness)

> Moses went out to meet his father-in-law [Jethro], bowed down, and kissed him. … Moses told his father-in-law all that the LORD had done to Pharaoh and to the Egyptians for Israel's sake, all the hardship that had come upon them on the way, and how the LORD had delivered them. —Exodus 18:7–8

Moses had great respect for Jethro, his father-in-law. Again, the way he greeted Jethro showed his humility. Jethro was a priest, but the Bible does not say he served the God of Abraham, Isaac, and Israel. Other religions had priests to sacrifice to their gods, and priests sometimes acted as medical advisors and teachers. Up to that point, Jethro had only heard secondhand how God had delivered Israel. So Moses shared with Jethro a firsthand account of how God delivered the Israelites from Egypt and how He helped them through the difficulties of the wilderness journey with God thus far.

Our Earthly Journey with Jesus (Others Drawn to God through Witness)

> Many of the Samaritans of that city believed in [on (KJV)] Him [Jesus] because of the word of the woman who testified, "He told me all that I ever did." … Many more believed because of His own Word. Then they said to the woman, "Now we believe, not because of what you said, for we ourselves have heard Him and we know that this is indeed the Christ, the Savior of the world." —John 4:39–42

This woman, who had just been told by Jesus—a complete stranger to her—all she had ever done, went into the city to witness to others what Jesus had told her, that He was the Messiah they had been waiting for. Many believed on Jesus because of her witness. But when they heard Jesus' witness firsthand, many more believed with certainty that Jesus was the Savior of the world. They urged Him to stay, and for the next two days, He taught them.

What about You?

Witness means "eyewitness/firsthand account." Have you ever given a firsthand account to others (including your family) about all the Lord has done to deliver you from sin and what God has been doing in your life since He gave you salvation? God has chosen you, His instrument, to be His witness. First, be His mouthpiece and share His Word through devotionals like this; or emails, letters, postcards, social media, phone calls, and face-to-face encounters. Second, be God's hands and feet by giving a firsthand account of His love through helping your neighbor: the weak, poor, sick, downcast, imprisoned, and so on. The ways to witness are endless.

Prayer

Father in heaven, thank You for Jesus, Your Witness. Help us witness to our families and others through word and deed, by giving them a firsthand account of how You delivered us from sin and have met our daily needs since then. Your salvation for us is so incredible that we cannot help sharing it with whomever we meet. We are forever grateful! In Jesus' name we pray, amen.

Verse of the Week/Day

> We [Peter, James, and John] … were eyewitnesses of His majesty. For He received from God the Father, honor, and glory, when such a voice came to Him [Jesus] from the Excellent Glory: "This is My beloved Son, in whom I am well pleased." And we heard this voice which came from heaven when we were with Him [Jesus] on the holy mountain. —2 Peter 1:16–18

Devotional 29
Israel's Wilderness Journey with God (Testimony of God's Power)

> **Then** Jethro rejoiced for all the good which the LORD had done for Israel, whom He had delivered out of the hand of the Egyptians. **And Jethro said, …** "Now I know that the LORD is greater than all the gods; for in the very thing in which they behaved proudly; He was above them." —Exodus 18:9–11

After hearing Moses' firsthand account and seeing how God had delivered Israel, Jethro was moved to believe and responded, "Now I know that the LORD is greater than all the gods; … He was above them." With Moses' witness of God's deliverance of Israel, Jethro no longer just heard about God's power but also had a testimony because the evidence was clear to see. Evidence like two to three million people being led through the wilderness and thriving, manna from heaven every morning, water coming from the rock where no water was before, the cloud by day and fire by night, animals surviving where there was little grass to eat, and so on.

Our Earthly Journey with Jesus (Testimony of Christ's Power)

> Jesus said to them, "Fill the water pots with water." And they filled them up to the brim. … When the master of the feast had tasted the water that was made wine, and did not know where it came from (but the servants … knew), the master … called the bridegroom. … And His disciples believed in [on (KJV)] Him. —John 2:7–11

The disciples and servants had just witnessed Jesus' first miracle and realized His true identity—His glory and sovereignty. They knew that the wine just a short time before had been water. Their response was belief that Jesus, whom they had been promised would come, was the Savior. Many of these people had been taught scripture from their youth and told about a Messiah who was coming to rescue them. This miracle must have been an amazing thing to them and proof that Jesus must be the Messiah they were waiting for, though they may have thought He would deliver them from the bondage of Rome and not the bondage of their sins.

What about You?
Testimony means "evidence/an outward sign/proof." Have you ever thought of yourself as a miracle of God? The transformation from being a spiritually dead person in sin into a spiritually alive person *in Christ* is the greatest miracle God has ever performed. You are the evidence of the joy of His salvation, the proof of the sovereignty and power of God, miraculously performed in you through His Holy Spirit. You *are* the miracle God has performed, the testimony of God's power to the world! Share yourself, with the Holy Spirit's help, so others may experience that same joy and salvation.

Prayer
Father in heaven, we acknowledge that You have accomplished the greatest miracle ever, making us spiritually alive *in Christ* after being spiritually dead in sin. We are the testimony and evidence of your power, the proof of Your sovereignty and salvation. With Your Holy Spirit, help us share with and show our family, friends, and others our testimony so they may experience the joy of salvation we have *in Christ*. In Jesus' name we pray, amen.

Verse of the Week/Day

> "When the Helper comes, whom I [Jesus] shall send to you from the Father, the Spirit of Truth who proceeds from the Father, He will testify of Me. And you also will bear witness [give testimony/show evidence], because you have been with Me from the beginning." —John 15:26–27

Devotional 30
Israel's Wilderness Journey with God (Moses Acknowledges His Weakness)

> Moses sat to judge the people; and the people stood … from morning until evening. … Moses' father-in-law [Jethro] said to him, "The thing that you do is not good. Both you and these people … will surely wear yourselves out. … You are not able to perform it by yourself. … Show them the way … and the work they must do." … So Moses heeded the voice of his father-in-law and did all that he had said. —Exodus 18:13–24

Within a day, Jethro observed that Moses was taking on all the problems of the people by himself. Perhaps Moses thought that he alone had been taught all the statutes and laws of God, so he alone, and no one else, could be a judge. But Jethro told Moses that he would wear out both himself and the people. He advised Moses to teach the people God's Law with the help of others. By heeding Jethro, he acknowledged his weaknesses and limitations as a human being. He began to share the responsibility of judging, teaching those helping him how to deal with the minor issues the people had, while he continued to judge the more complex, weightier matters; things that needed to be taken to the LORD for His advice.

Our Earthly Journey with Jesus (Confessing Our Weaknesses/Sin)

> Jesus said, … "Simon [Peter], … do you love Me?" … He said to Him, "Yes, Lord; You know that I love You." … He said to him … a second time, "Simon [Peter], … do you love Me?" He said to Him, "Yes, Lord; You know that I love You." He said to him the third time, "Simon [Peter], … do you love Me?" Peter … said to Him, "Lord, You know all things; You know that I love You." —John 21:15–17

On the night before His crucifixion, Jesus told Peter he would deny Him three times, but Peter said he would never deny Him. When Peter was confronted three times for being one of Jesus' disciples during Jesus' trial, he denied knowing Jesus every single time for fear of being arrested also. So after His resurrection, Jesus confronted Peter and asked him three times if he genuinely loved Him, the same number of times Peter had denied Him. Peter was extremely sorrowful and confessed his weakness—sin. Jesus forgave him and restored him to the shared responsibility of apostleship with the other disciples.

What about You?
Acknowledge means "to confess." Sometimes, God sends others to you to point out your limitations and sin when you try to do things on your own. Have you listened, confessing your sin/weaknesses to God, and then to others?

Prayer
Father in heaven, we acknowledge that we try to do things on our own that we are not capable of doing, including confessing our sin. By Your Holy Spirit, help us confess our sin and acknowledge our weaknesses daily to You first of all. Then with the comfort and support from Your Word, ask for assistance from others when there are situations we cannot handle on our own. Thank You, Holy Spirit, that You are our constant help, even though we do not always recognize that. In Jesus' name we pray, amen.

Verse of the Week/Day

> Seeing then that we have a great High Priest, … Jesus, … let us hold fast to our confession. For we do not have a High Priest who … [is unable to] sympathize with our weaknesses, but was in all points tempted as we are, yet without sin. Let us therefore come boldly to the throne of grace, that we may obtain mercy, and find grace to help us in time of need. —Hebrews 4:14–16

Devotional 31
Israel's Wilderness Journey with God (God's Advice—Seventy Judges—Filled with the Spirit)
>[Jethro said,] … "Select … able men, such as fear God, men of truth, hating covetousness;" … —Exodus 18:21

>The LORD said to Moses; "Gather to Me seventy men of the elders of Israel, … I will take of the Spirit that is upon you and will put the same upon them." —Numbers 11:16–17a

Jethro's advice was good because Moses needed help judging. But Moses forgot to do one thing, to bring Jethro's advice before the LORD in prayer. The judges appointed were not filled with the Spirit. So when the people began complaining again about their needs not being met, Moses, being frustrated, prayed to the LORD for help. According to Numbers 11, God told Moses to gather the seventy elders—one from each family group—and come before Him. He would place His Holy Spirit in them as He had done with Moses. As God's appointed judges—filled with His Spirit, they were able to apply God's Law and resolve the people's grievances.

Our Earthly Journey with Jesus (Jesus' Advice—Follow Me—Be Filled with the Spirit)
>He [Jesus] said to him [Peter], "Follow Me." Then Peter, turning around, saw the disciple whom Jesus loved. … Peter, seeing him, said to Jesus, "But Lord, what about this man?" Jesus said, "If I will that he remain until I come, what is that to you? You follow Me." —John 21:19–22

After Peter confessed his sin, telling Jesus how much he loved Him, Jesus tested Peter by revealing to him what kind of death he would die, one that would possibly be on a cross. Then Jesus said to Peter, "Follow Me" (John 21:19 NKJV). Perhaps out of fear and wanting to know if others had to be as committed, Peter asked Jesus about how John was going to die. Jesus told Peter not to be concerned about what God had in store for John and repeated, "You follow Me." (John 21:22 NKJV). On Pentecost, the Holy Spirit filled Peter and helped him follow Jesus without fear, and boldly preach His Word to all those God had brought to Jerusalem.

What about You?
Advice means "instruction." If you are like most human beings, you want to know what the future holds. Perhaps you want God to speak to you directly as Jesus did with Peter, or some sign that shows you exactly what will occur, or some communication telling you precisely what to expect. But God does not work that way. God's instruction for you is in His Word. He wants you to bring every decision and concern to Him in prayer first, and then by faith, to follow the advice in His Word with obedience, which only the Holy Spirit can help you with. If you knew each day what was in store for you, you would take the credit and say you had accomplished *your* goals. But God wants you to be dependent on Him alone. All you need to know is that—filled with His Holy Spirit—God will be with you. You *must* follow Jesus.

Prayer
Father in heaven, we confess that we want to control our lives so that we know what to expect each day. But You want us to depend on You, to be instruments *played* by You. By faith, help us bring every decision and concern to you in prayer. Then with Your Holy Spirit, help us follow and obey the instructions You give us in Your Word. In Jesus' name we pray, amen.

Verse of the Week/Day
>"Receive, please, instruction from His [God's] mouth, and lay up His words in your heart." —Job 22:22

Devotional 32
Israel's Wilderness Journey with God (Through Moses—God Chose Israel to Be Holy)
> The LORD called to him [Moses] … saying, … "Tell the children of Israel: You have seen what I did to the Egyptians, and how I bore you on eagles' wings and brought you to Myself. Now therefore, if you will indeed obey My voice and keep My covenant, then you shall be a special treasure to Me above all people; for all the earth is Mine. And you shall be to Me a kingdom of priests and a holy nation." —Exodus 19:3–6

God was repeating His covenant with Moses and the people of Israel that He would be their God and they would be His people, His chief treasure. It is a special thing to be called the chief treasure of God. Up to that point, Israel did not deserve to have that favor, that grace. Still, God carried them because He had chosen them beforehand to be His treasure—His holy people—out of all the other peoples on earth.

The Israelites were not allowed to look upon God's holiness, so He came in a thick cloud to accomplish Israel's sanctification, bringing His message through Moses—who had been filled with His Holy Spirit.

Our Earthly Journey with Jesus (Through Jesus—God Chose Us to Be Holy)
> "You are already clean, [made holy], because of the Word which I have spoken to you. … You did not choose Me, but I chose you and appointed you, that you should go and bear fruit." —John 15:3 & 16

When Jesus told the disciples that they were already clean (holy), though He had not yet died on the cross for them, He was referring to the adoption and election that God had predestined before time had begun. We human beings do not understand how God determines that; we just know it is true because God's Word—Jesus Christ—says we are clean. Isaiah 55:11 says that when God speaks, His Word does not come back empty but accomplishes what it was sent out to do. By grace, not merit, God chose us as His chief treasure, making us holy and adopting us to bear fruit through Jesus.

What about You?
Chose means "elected/adopted." Though you do not deserve His favor (grace), God through Christ chose you to be His special treasure. Through the message of His Word, He adopted you to be holy, obedient, and fruit-bearing. According to John 15, holiness, obedience, and bearing fruit means to abide in His Word through prayer, to give of yourself to others in service, to endure persecution from the world, and to witness to the world about God's great love for them.

Prayer
Father in heaven, thank You for choosing us to be Your special treasure. Only through Jesus can we be holy and bear fruit. By the Holy Spirit's power, help us abide in Your Word through prayer, give ourselves to others in service, endure persecution from the world, and witness to others about Your great love for us. In the holy name of Jesus we pray, amen.

Verse of the Week/Day
> Blessed be the God and Father of our Lord Jesus Christ, who has blessed us with every spiritual blessing in the heavenly places in Christ, just as He chose us in Him before the foundation of the world, that we should be holy and without blame before Him in love, having predestined us to adoption as sons [and daughters] by Jesus Christ to Himself, according to the good pleasure of His will, to the praise of the glory of His grace.
> —Ephesians 1:3–6

Devotional 33
Israel's Wilderness Journey with God (Israel Responsible for Its Disobedience—God's Mercy)

> Moses returned to the LORD and said, … "Yet now, if You will forgive their sin, but if not, I pray, blot me out." … The LORD said to Moses, "Whoever has sinned against Me, I will blot them out of My book." … So the LORD plagued the people, because of what they did with the calf which Aaron made. —Exodus 32:31–35

Moses was on Mount Sinai for forty days and nights to receive God's instruction and commandments. The children of Israel grew tired of waiting for Moses to come back down from the mountain, so they asked Aaron to make an idol of a golden calf similar to what the Egyptians worshipped. Because of their sin, God's anger burned against them. He told Moses that He was going to destroy those who had sinned. When God said He would blot out of His book those who had sinned, Moses said, "Forgive their sin, but if not, blot me out" instead. Moses, knowing God was merciful, loved these people so much that he was willing to die for the children of Israel, sacrificing his life in their place. God heard Moses' plea, mercifully answered Moses' prayer, and did not blot those who had sinned out of His Book of Life, but instead graciously sent a plague to punish them.

Our Earthly Journey with Jesus (Responsible for Our Disobedience—Jesus' Mercy)

> The scribes and Pharisees brought to Him [Jesus] a woman caught in adultery. —John 8:3a

> When they continued asking Him, He raised Himself up and said to them, "He who is without sin among you, let him throw a stone at her first." … Then those who heard it, being convicted by their conscience, went out one by one, beginning with the oldest even to the last. … He [Jesus] said to her, "Woman, where are those accusers of yours? Has no one condemned you?" She said, "No one, Lord." And Jesus said to her, "Neither do I condemn you; go and sin no more." —John 8:7–11

This scripture is probably one of the most gracious and merciful passages in the Bible. The Pharisees were trying to find some accusation they could bring against Jesus, so they tried to corner Him with this woman who had been caught in the very act of adultery and punishable according to Moses' law by stoning to death. Jesus knew their motivations, so He told those who were without sin to cast the first stone at her. One by one, her accusers left because they were convicted of their own sin. By grace/mercy, Jesus forgave the woman. He soon paid for her sins on the cross, blotting them out forever. The woman was humiliated, but she no longer had to face condemnation because of her sin.

What about You?
Responsible means "guilty/punishable." When you sin against God, you are guilty, punishable by eternal death. But God loved you so much that He gave Jesus, who willingly sacrificed His life in your place so that you would not be blotted out of His presence forever, but by His grace and mercy, be forgiven. No longer condemned, you have eternal life and will never be forsaken by God, though you still have to face the consequences of sin in this life.

Prayer
Father in heaven, thank You that *in Jesus* we are no longer condemned but by Your grace/mercy are forgiven. In Jesus' name we pray, amen.

Verse of the Week/Day

> There is … now no condemnation to those who are in Christ Jesus. —Romans 8:1a

Devotional 34
Israel's Wilderness Journey with God (Israel Belonged to God—No Covenants with Canaan)

He [the LORD] said: … "Before all your people I will do marvels such as have not been done in all the earth, nor in any nation; and all the people among whom you are, shall see the work of the LORD. For it is an awesome thing that I will do with you. Observe what I command you this day … lest you make a covenant with the inhabitants of the land where you are going." —Exodus 34:10–12

The awesome thing that God is talking about is His adoption of the Israelites. They were His people, His family. He dwelt among them on their journey in the wilderness and into the land of Canaan, making them His inheritance despite their unworthiness. His faithfulness and love would never leave them. Therefore, God cautioned the Israelites to obey His covenant with them and not serve other gods or make covenants with the people of the land where they were going. Canaan's way of life led to sin and death. Israel was not to take part in their idol worship. In fact, God told the Israelites to destroy Canaan's idols. If not, future generations would be affected and eventually fall away from the LORD.

Our Earthly Journey with Jesus (We Belong to Jesus—No Covenants with the World)

"I [Jesus] am the door of the sheep. All who ever came before Me are thieves and robbers. If anyone enters by Me, he [they] will be saved, and will go in and out and find pasture. The thief does not come except to steal, … kill, and … destroy. I have come that they may have life, and that they may have it more abundantly."

—John 10:7–10

Jesus told His followers not to covenant with (follow the ways of) the world but flee from it because they steal, kill, and destroy, which leads to sin and death. We entered the covenant of grace with God through the door—Jesus. He gives overflowing life by saving those who are drawn by God to Him. He owns us twice over. We belong to Him.

What about You?
Covenant means "a promise between two parties." In Genesis 15, God made a covenant with Abraham, but He knew that Abraham could not fulfill his part of the covenant. So God, by Himself, went through the sacrifice that Abraham had prepared, pledging to be Abraham's God; and then in the fullness of time, fulfilled Abraham's part of the covenant through Christ. Now, you are under the new covenant of grace.

You, like the Israelites, covenanted with (followed the ways of) the world, so God took it upon Himself to fulfill His part of the covenant with you, being a faithful God, and your part of the covenant with Him, through Jesus' obedient sacrifice on the cross. You belong to Him twice over. He created you, then after you sinned, He bought you back with His blood.

Prayer
Father in heaven, thank You for the covenant of grace. You faithfully fulfilled Your part of the covenant (being our faithful God) and our part of the covenant (obedience) through Jesus' obedient sacrifice—dying for our sins on the cross. Jesus, You made us, then bought us back with Your blood when we faithlessly disobeyed You and covenanted with the world. Father, forgive us. By the Holy Spirit's power, fill us with Jesus' righteousness so we may have life in abundance. In His name we pray, amen.

Verse of the Week/Day
He [Jesus] said, "Behold, I have come to do Your will, O God." He takes away the first [covenant of works—our righteousness] that He may establish the second [covenant of grace—His righteousness]. —Hebrews 10:9

Devotional 35
Israel's Wilderness Journey with God (Moses Taught the People God's Word)

> When Moses came down from Mount Sinai (and the two tablets of the Testimony were in Moses' hand), … the skin of his face shown, … and they were afraid to come near him. Then Moses called to them, and Aaron and all the rulers of the congregation returned to him; and Moses talked with them. … The children of Israel came near, and He gave them as commandments all that the LORD had spoken with him on Mount Sinai.
> —Exodus 34:29–32

God wrote with His own finger the Ten Commandments on two tablets of stone. Then Moses brought them down from Mount Sinai to the children of Israel. At first, the people were afraid and ran away from Moses because his face was so brilliant after being in God's presence for a lengthy period of time. But Moses called them back, drawing them near to hear God's Word and teaching the people orally the commands God had given him. None of the Bible had been written up to this point, only the Ten Commandments were written on stone. Maybe there were some genealogies written down, but most everything else was handed down from generation to generation orally. Moses became the lawgiver along with the help of Joshua, who was being prepared to be the next leader of Israel, and taught God's knowledge/commands to Israel.

Our Earthly Journey with Jesus (Jesus Teaches Us His Word)

> [Jesus speaking] "It is written in the prophets, 'And they shall all be taught by God.' … Everyone who has heard and learned from the Father comes to Me." —John 6:45

John 1 says that at first, Jesus' own people (the Jews) did not receive Him. Since they did not come on their own, the Father began drawing them near to Himself through His Word—Jesus Christ. Jesus, who was sent by God and knew God's will, went to the Jews. He called them to follow Him and taught them the Truth so all who received Him—those who believed on Him— would have eternal life. Through His Word, God began to penetrate their hearts of stone, and made them into hearts of flesh, so they could hear and understand what Jesus taught them.

What about You?

To *teach* means "to impart knowledge or understanding." Like Israel and the Jews, you do not come to God on your own either. God draws you to Himself through Jesus, His Word, putting Himself in you and writing His Word on your heart by the powerful work of the Holy Spirit. His Word (Jesus) is always in you, imparting knowledge and understanding, so you will know how to live in obedience on this journey through life with Him.

Prayer

Father, thank You for drawing us to Yourself when we refused to come to You, and for miraculously transforming our hearts of stone into hearts of flesh. You have written Your Word in our hearts to keep us from sinning against You. Through the Holy Spirit's power, help us understand increasingly who You are and give us the knowledge to continue this journey through life with You obediently. In Jesus' name we pray, amen.

Verse of the Week/Day

> "I will give you a new heart and put a new spirit within you; I will take the heart of stone out of your flesh and give you a heart of flesh. I will put My Spirit within you and cause you to walk in My statutes, and you will keep My judgments and do [obey] them." —Ezekiel 36:26–27

Devotional 36
Israel's Wilderness Journey with God (Serving God Wholeheartedly)

> Then everyone came whose heart was stirred, and everyone whose spirit was willing, and they brought the LORD's offering for the work of the tabernacle of meeting, for all its service, and for the holy garments. They came, both men and women, as many as had a willing heart. —Exodus 35:21–22

Moses asked the Israelites to bring wholehearted offerings for the LORD's work on the tabernacle. Out of grateful hearts, the people gave materials and labor because the LORD had stirred them; heart, soul, mind, and body, and made them willing and able to serve Him by what He had done for them. The tabernacle and its articles of worship were built by the men with precious metals such as gold, silver, and brass. It had curtains that the women skillfully spun of fine linen such as blue, scarlet, and purple silk. Goat's hair and animal skins were used to make clothing for the priests along with a special type of wood to make furniture. Precious stones, oil for light and anointing, and incense were also given. God made His dwelling in the tabernacle, a physical building, where the children of Israel worshipped. This was where they offered to God sacrifices of animals for sin and where they heard the law read.

Our Earthly Journey with Jesus (Serving Jesus Wholeheartedly)

> Jesus came to Bethany, where Lazarus was who had been dead, whom He had raised from the dead. There they made Him a supper; and Martha served, but Lazarus was one of those who sat at the table with Him. Then Mary took a pound of very costly oil of spikenard, anointed the feet of Jesus, and wiped His feet with her hair. And the house was filled with the fragrance of the oil. —John 12:1–3

Some of Jesus' closest friends were Lazarus, Mary, and Martha. They lived right outside of Jerusalem in Bethany. Shortly before Jesus was to be crucified, He and the disciples were invited to their house for a meal. Lazarus, who had been raised from the dead, was hosting the meal, and was seated at the table. Martha, out of a heart of love for Jesus, did what she knew best and served the meal. Mary, with a heart stirred with love and thanksgiving for what Jesus had done for their family by raising Lazarus from the dead, poured expensive perfume on Jesus' feet, and wiped them with her hair. Each showed Jesus wholehearted thanksgiving in their own special way.

What about You?

Wholeheartedly means "enthusiastically, willingly, without reservation." Because Jesus has willingly given Himself to us, we are able to give in return. Have you given to Jesus—enthusiastically, willingly, and without reservation—yourself and all you have, for His service? God wants His church to serve with a willing heart, soul, mind, and body, so His kingdom may come, His will be done. Moved by love for what Jesus has done for you, will you wholeheartedly serve Him in your own special way?

Prayer

Father in heaven, by the power of the Holy Spirit, stir us to give wholeheartedly to You—willingly, without reservation—of ourselves and all we have for Your service. Thank You for making us unique, each able to serve You in our own special way. May Your kingdom come, and may Your will be done on earth as it is in heaven. In Jesus' name we pray, amen.

Verse of the Week/Day

> But God be thanked that though you were slaves of sin, yet you obeyed from the heart. … Having been set free from sin, you became slaves of righteousness. —Romans 6:17–18

Devotional 37
Israel's Wilderness Journey with God (Israel Designed the Tabernacle for Worship)
> All the work of the tabernacle of the tent of meeting was finished. … The children of Israel did according to all that the LORD had commanded Moses. … And they brought the tabernacle to Moses. … Then Moses looked over all the work, … and Moses blessed them. —Exodus 39:32–43

God had prepared the hearts of the Israelites to carry out the plans He had for them to worship Him. You might wonder where they found the material to build the tabernacle and its furnishings, especially in a barren wilderness. Remember that when they left Egypt, they were given everything needed for the journey—jewelry, clothes, perfume, items made of wood, precious metals, etc., along with their own animals. It says in Exodus 12:36 that they plundered the Egyptians.

The LORD provided everything they needed for the tent and outer court—the ark and poles, furniture and accessories, lampstand, utensils, oil, altars for incense and offerings, and garments for the priests and Levites. All this was fashioned and made by those whom God had gifted. They obeyed all that the LORD had commanded them to do, serving Him and each other. When finished, they brought it before the LORD. Through Moses, God blessed them.

Our Earthly Journey with Jesus (Jesus Designed the Heart for Worship)
> [Jesus] "The hour is coming, and now is, when the true worshipers will worship the Father in spirit and truth; for the Father is seeking such to worship Him." —John 4:23–24

We no longer worship from an outer tabernacle but from an inner tabernacle—the heart, the place Jesus designed with His own hands. With His Word—Jesus Christ—in us by the power of the Holy Spirit, we can obediently worship Him wherever we are, in Spirit and Truth.

What about You?
Worship means "giving highest praise, devotion." Are you giving yourself to the service of God? Is it coming from a devoted heart? Do you love Him and others because you have to or because you want to? If you worship God because you have to, it is not coming from the heart. If you worship Him because you want to, it is coming from a grateful, devoted heart. Giving worship spiritually from the heart displays obedience and is what God has commanded of you. Obedience brings God's blessings, not only to you, but also to all who serve and whom are served.

Prayer
Father in heaven, thank You for building Your new Tabernacle (Jesus Christ) in us by the power of the Holy Spirit. We are grateful that we are the permanent place where you dwell, not created with human hands but by Your almighty power. By Your grace, help us to worship You obediently only in Spirit and Truth, and love You with devoted, obedient hearts You have designed. Together, You have gifted us in so many ways to love You first and then to love and serve each other. Accomplish Your will in and through us as a community of believers. In Jesus' name we pray, amen.

Verse of the Week/Day
> For we are the circumcision, who worship God in the Spirit, rejoice in Christ Jesus, and have no confidence in the flesh. … Not having my own righteousness, which is from the law, but that which is through faith in [the faith of (KJV)] Christ, the righteousness which is from God by faith. —Philippians 3:3–9

Devotional 38
Israel's Wilderness Journey with God (The Sacrificial Lamb—No Broken Bones)
> Then the LORD spoke to Moses, saying, "Speak to the children of Israel, saying: … keep the LORD's Passover. … They shall eat it [a lamb] with unleavened bread and bitter herbs. They shall leave none of it until morning, nor break one of its bones. … The man [person] who is clean and is not on a journey, and ceases to keep the Passover, that same person shall be cut off from among his people." —Numbers 9:9–13

Every year on the fourteenth day of the first month, the children of Israel were to celebrate the Passover in remembrance of their rescue from their bondage in Egypt by sacrificing a lamb and eating unleavened bread and bitter herbs. The sacrificial lamb symbolized Christ, so no bones were to be broken when the lamb sacrificially gave its life for the partakers, the Israelites.

All Israel was to take part in the Passover Feast. If they could not keep the Passover because of uncleanness or perhaps were gone on a journey, they were to celebrate the Passover on the fourteenth day of the second month. If they did not keep the Passover, they were considered outcasts because they did not partake (share) in the community of God, the Israelites.

Our Earthly Journey with Jesus (Jesus, the Sacrificial Lamb—No Broken Bones)
> The Jews asked Pilate that their legs might be broken, and that they might be taken away. Then the soldiers came and broke the legs of the first and of the other who was crucified with Him. But when they came to Jesus and saw that He was already dead, they did not break His legs. … These things were done that the Scripture should be fulfilled, "Not one of His bones shall be broken." —John 19:31–36

Jesus died around three p.m. In three hours, the Sabbath day would begin. According to Jewish law, no bodies were to be left hanging on the Sabbath, so the Jews asked Pilate for permission to take down the bodies of Jesus and the two thieves crucified with Him. If anyone were still alive, their legs were broken so that death would come quicker. The soldiers did not break the bones of Jesus because He had already sacrificially given His life for us. Let me repeat this statement. Jesus' life was not taken; He had freely given it up for us. We know that because in Luke 23:46 (NKJV) we read, "Father, into Your hands I commit [give] my spirit [life]." Then Jesus died. The two thieves' legs were broken, and their lives were taken from them.

What about You?
Sacrifice means "to offer up or give up." Jesus offered up His life to pay for your sins as the sacrificial Lamb. Have you participated in the celebration of the Lord's Supper, remembering His broken body and His shed blood for the forgiveness of your sins? Have you eaten the Lamb (been filled with the holiness of His Word), giving Him all your praise and worship, honor and glory, and then offered your life as a living sacrifice for His service—serving (sharing) in His body, the church?

Prayer
Father in heaven, thank You for giving us Jesus, who sacrificially gave His life for us on the cross for our sin. Help us offer our bodies as living sacrifices, having eaten and been filled with the holiness of Your Word so we may serve You and Your body, the church. May Your will alone be accomplished on earth as it is in heaven. In Jesus' name we pray, amen.

Verse of the Week/Day
> I beseech you therefore, brethren [and sisters], by the mercies of God, that you present your bodies a living sacrifice, holy, acceptable to God, which is your reasonable service. —Romans 12:1

Devotional 39
Israel's Wilderness Journey with God (Ark Embodied God's Presence—Follow the Ark/God)

The ark of the covenant of the LORD went before them for the three days' journey, to search out a resting place for them. —Numbers 10:33

The ark contained the two stone tablets with the Ten Commandments written by the finger of God. It was the place where God's presence and His Word, the Law, were. Whenever God wanted the Israelites to move to a different location, His presence would lift off the tabernacle, the priests would pick up the ark with His Word—the Law—in it, and the Israelites would follow the ark until the cloud of pillar and fire (His presence) would stop. Then the tabernacle would be set up, the ark would be put in its resting place in the inner room (the holy of holies), and the presence of the LORD would again come down into the ark. Whether they stayed in a place for a while or moved, God's presence was always near to keep a constant watch and give them rest. That rest was God's reward for obedience in following Him and His Word.

Our Earthly Journey with Jesus (Jesus Embodies God's Presence—Follow the Spirit/Jesus)

"Whoever serves Me [Jesus] must follow Me; and where I am, my servant also will be. My Father will honor the one who serves Me." —John 12:26 (NIV)

Just like the LORD commanded the Israelites of the Old Testament to obediently follow Him, Jesus wants His disciples to follow (obey) Him and be where He wants them to be. A servant does not wander off but is where the Master is. That can happen only when we, with the Holy Spirit's present help, follow Him, obey His Word, and walk in His service. God honors us when we serve Him. Through the power of the Holy Spirit in us, He gives our heart, soul, mind, and body a resting place now and in eternity.

What about You?

Presence means "state of being near, nearness of God." God did not leave the Israelites alone. He was always near. The Israelites saw the nearness of God all around them because His presence was in the ark at the tabernacle, the pillar of cloud, and the pillar of fire. Only Aaron, Moses, and the elders had God's presence in them so that they could be instruments of leadership. You too have Christ's presence all around you but especially in you by the Holy Spirit. Follow Jesus. *In Him* you will find a resting place.

Prayer

Father in heaven, thank You for giving us Your Spirit—Jesus' constant presence all around us and especially in us. We pray that we may always be instruments who walk by faith and follow Jesus, thankfully loving, praising, and serving You so that we may have a resting place for our whole being—heart, soul, mind, and body. Help us not wander off on our own but follow where the Spirit moves us to go. In Jesus' name we pray, amen.

Verse of the Week/Day

Where can I go from your Spirit? Where can I flee from your presence? If I go up to the heavens, you are there; if I make my bed in the depths, you are there. If I rise on the wings of the dawn, if I settle on the far side of the sea, even there your hand will guide me, your right hand will hold me fast. If I say, "Surely the darkness will hide me and the light become night around me," even the darkness will not be dark to you; the night will shine like the day, for darkness is as light to you. —Psalm 139:7–12 (NIV)

Devotional 40
Israel's Wilderness Journey with God (Rabble/Rebels—Children of Unknown Fathers)

> Now the mixed multitude [the rabble] who were among them yielded to intense craving; so the children of Israel also wept again and said: "Who will give us meat to eat?" … The people went about and gathered it [manna], ground it on millstones or beat it in the mortar, cooked it in pans, and made cakes of it; and its taste was like the taste of pastry prepared with oil. —Numbers 11:4–8

Genealogies (family trees/known ancestors) were especially important in the Bible. The Israelites knew exactly what family they belonged to. Others had left Egypt with Israel (Exodus 12:38); they were the rabble. No one knows who these people were aside from being Egyptians. Still, their fathers were unknown. The rabble were sick and tired of having the same food every day, so they tried to prepare the manna their way instead of leaving it the way God had intended it to be. They gathered manna and made it into cakes that tasted like olive oil. According to Exodus 16:31, the manna God sent tasted like wafers made with honey. By their own doing, they loathed it and so rebelled, then caused all the people to rebel. To stop the rebellion, God swiftly sent judgment, and the rabble died from a plague.

Our Earthly Journey with Jesus (Barabbas/Rebellious—Son of Unknown Father)

> [Pilate said], "You have a custom that I should release someone to you at the Passover. Do you therefore want me to release to you the King of the Jews?" Then they all cried again, saying, "Not this Man, but Barabbas!" Now Barabbas was a robber. —John 18:39–40

The name *Barabbas* means "rebellious, son of his unknown father." Barabbas was a notorious rebel and a prisoner of Rome. Apparently, he was not happy with the state of affairs he found himself and his nation in, so he led a murderous rebellion against the authorities. The Bible does not say who Barabbas' father was or what family Barabbas came from. The Jews chose to set him free rather than Jesus, the sinless Savior and righteous Judge of the world, the name everyone will someday know and confess as the King of Kings and Lord of Lords.

What about You?
Rabble means "mob that stirs up hatred, rebellion." This is the way of the world, and sometimes we can get caught up in it, wanting something we do not have. Instead of being content with what God gives you, are you sometimes rebellious, discontented, and ungrateful for His blessings? Has it caused others to be dissatisfied and disobedient also? If so, have you humbly asked God to forgive you and fill you with Christ's obedience? Someday, the rabble, those who stir up hatred and rebellion, will die and be remembered for their disobedience, then forgotten.

Prayer
Father in heaven, You have given us so many blessings that we are not grateful for. Forgive us for getting caught up in worldly, rebellious ways. Thank you for putting in us the humility and obedience of Christ. Cause His obedience to pour forth from us so that the world may know and believe that Jesus is truly the King of Kings and Lord of Lords. In His name we pray, amen.

Verse of the Week/Day
> … God also has highly exalted Him and given Him the name which is above every name, that at the name of Jesus every knee should bow, of those in heaven, … of those on earth, and of those under the earth, and that every tongue should confess that Jesus Christ is Lord, to the glory of God the Father. —Philippians 2:9–11

Devotional 41
Israel's Wilderness Journey with God (Joshua/Caleb Report—Victory Foretold)
> But Joshua … and Caleb, who were among those who had spied out the land, tore their clothes; … "do not rebel against the LORD, nor fear the people of the land, … the LORD is with us." —Numbers 14:6–9

Just before the Israelites were freed from bondage in Egypt, God foretold the people through Moses in Exodus 13:5 that He would bring them into Canaan, a land flowing with milk and honey. They were at the southern border of Canaan. Twelve spies, one from each tribe, went into the land to search it out. Ten of them came back with a bad report and said there were giants in the land they would not be able to conquer. Two of them, Joshua and Caleb, came back with a good report and urged the people not to rebel against the LORD because the LORD had promised them victory. But the Israelites did not believe them and rebelled against God and Moses. God had kept every promise He had made with them and had taken care of every need in miraculous ways all through their wilderness journey with Him. They would soon find out the cost of unbelief.

Our Earthly Journey with Jesus (Disciple Report—Victory Foretold)
> Jesus said, … "I am the resurrection and the life, … whoever lives and believes in [on (ASV)] Me shall never die [spiritually]." —John 11:25–26

> Now Thomas … was not with them [the disciples] when Jesus came. … He said to them, "Unless I see … His hands, and … His side, I will not believe." —John 20:24–25

When the disciples told Thomas that they had seen Jesus alive, he would not believe them. He and the disciples were present when Jesus told Mary and Martha (when Lazarus had died) that He was the Resurrection and the Life and would rise victoriously from the dead. Thomas would not believe unless he saw Jesus alive and felt His wounds. His unbelief cost him another week of doubt and sadness.

What about You?
Foretold means "to predict a future event." One future event remains—Jesus' second coming. God has promised you that Jesus is coming again to victoriously take you to be with Him forever. When you are *in Christ*, you are made alive spiritually. Though you will die physically and return to the earth where you came from, your living spirit will be transported to heaven to be with Jesus. When (not if) Jesus comes back again to judge the world, your body will be resurrected from the dead and will be reunited with your soul/spirit. Do you believe Jesus is coming back? Or do you have doubts because of scoffers who say that it has been two centuries since the promise was made. Believe His Word! God's promises have never failed—never!

Prayer
Father in heaven, thank You for keeping every promise You made in Your Word. Jesus, we believe You will come again even though the world scoffs at us and insults us with words and actions of disbelief. Help us not doubt when we are afraid but patiently wait for You to come and take us someday to live with You—where righteousness dwells—victoriously forever. In Jesus' name we pray, amen.

Verse of the Week/Day
> Scoffers will come … saying, "Where is the promise of His coming?" … We, according to His promise, look for new heavens and a new earth. —2 Peter 3:3–13

Devotional 42
Israel's Wilderness Journey with God (Spent Forty Years in the Wilderness)
"As I live," says the LORD, "just as you have spoken, ... you who have complained [sinned] against Me, shall fall [die] in this wilderness, ... your entire number, from twenty years old and above, except for Caleb ... and Joshua. ... Your little ones ... I will bring in, and they shall know [inhabit] the land which you have despised. You ... and Your sons [children] shall be ... in the wilderness forty years." —Numbers 14:28–33

Because the Israelites did not put their trust in God to bring them into Canaan, God told them that all who were twenty and older would die in the wilderness except Joshua and Caleb, who were going into the land of promise because they believed God's Word. Israel would have to stay in the wilderness for forty years—the rest of their lives, suffering the consequences of their sin and unbelief. After the forty years, God would bring their children and grandchildren into the land promised to them through Moses. Some people disobeyed God and tried on their own to enter Canaan anyway, but God defeated them through those who inhabited the land, and they died in battle. When God promises or decrees something, it always comes to pass. Those Israelites found that out the hard way.

Our Earthly Journey with Jesus (Spend a Lifetime in a Sinful World)
"If the world hates you, you know that it hated Me [Jesus] before it hated you. If you were of the world, the world would love its own. ... If they persecuted Me, they will also persecute you. If they kept My Word, they will keep [listen to] yours also. ... They have no excuse for their sin." —John 15:18–22

Because sin came into the world through Adam and Eve, all people will live their lives in this sinful world and die when their time on earth is fulfilled. But with Christ, Christians have the sure hope and promise of eternal life. Christians will have to face trouble and persecution from the world before they will be taken to be with Him and live forever in the land of promise, heaven.

Those without Christ have no hope at all and will be eternally separated from God when they die unless His Word penetrates their hearts. Otherwise, they will have no excuse for their sin, and even though they may try on their own, they will be turned away, never to enter heaven.

What about You?
Lifetime means "the period from birth to death." You too, because of the consequences of sin, will live your lives in this sinful world and die when your time here is fulfilled. But if you are *in Christ*, death is only temporary. Because you know He lives, you also have the sure hope of eternal life! God has chosen you to be His instrument to bring the good news of salvation to the world, so you are going to be persecuted by those who are spiritually dead in sin, those lost unless transformed by God.

Prayer
Lord Jesus, thank You for dying for our sins and giving us the sure hope of eternal life as we live and die in this sinful world. Use us to bring Your good news of salvation to the world even if we have to face persecution and death, so others can be saved and not be turned away from the land of promise, heaven. We look forward to living with You forever. In Your name we pray, amen.

Verse of the Week/Day
He who [Whoever] has the Son has life, he who [whoever] does not ... does not have life. —1 John 5:12

Devotional 43
Israel's Wilderness Journey with God (Speak to the Rock to Quench Thirst)

> Now there was no water for the congregation; so they gathered together against Moses and Aaron. … So Moses and Aaron … fell on their faces. … Then the LORD spoke to Moses, saying, "Take the rod; you and your brother Aaron gather the congregation together. Speak to the rock before their eyes, and it will yield its water."
>
> —Numbers 20:2–8

The children of Israel complained to Moses about thirst again, so God told Moses He would use a rock to quench their thirst. This is the second time God asked Moses to use a rock to give the people of Israel water, but instead of striking it with the rod, God asked Moses to speak to it because the Rock (Yahweh) had already been struck earlier at Mount Sinai/Horeb. All that was needed now was God's Word to bring forth water. So why did God ask Moses to take the staff? To see if Moses would obey, and because he was God's spokesman, to display God as a testimony in front of all the people as merciful yet again, that by His Spoken Word alone He would quench the thirst of the Israelites.

Our Earthly Journey with Jesus (Words of Eternal Life Quench Thirst)

> From that time many of His disciples went back and walked with Him no more. Then Jesus said to the twelve, "Do you also want to go away?" … Peter answered Him, "Lord, to whom shall we go? You have the words of eternal life. Also we have come to believe and know that You are the Christ, the Son of the living God."
>
> —John 6:66–69

As has been mentioned before, many of Jesus' followers pursued Him because He took care of their physical needs. But when Jesus gave them of Himself, the Word of eternal life that would quench their thirst spiritually, and claimed to be the Son of God who would deliver them from sin, many left Him. Jesus tested His faithful disciples by asking if they also wanted to leave. Peter testified that Jesus was the Christ, God's Son, and that they would be lost, dead without His "Words of eternal life."

What about You?

Word means "special revelation from God." Jesus was struck (crucified) once upon the cross. All that is needed now is the Word of God to quench the thirst of the body and soul. When God created the world by His Word, it yielded food and water and quenched the needs of the body as it did for the Israelites. When Jesus, the Word of God, died for your sin, it yielded life and quenched the needs of the soul as it did for Jesus' disciples. Jesus' work of salvation was finished on the cross, once and for all who are *in Christ*. So as His spokesperson, bring the Word to everyone and let God speak in and through you. His Word has the power to quench the thirsty souls of those you interact with, and yield eternal life.

Prayer

Father in heaven, we know Jesus is the Christ, Your Son. Thank You for Jesus' sacrifice on the cross and His resurrection from the dead, once and for all who are *in Christ*. As Your spokespersons, speak Your Word of eternal life in and through us so that it may quench the thirst of our souls and other thirsty souls that need to come to You for forgiveness and thus receive eternal life. In Jesus' name we pray, amen.

Verse of the Week/Day

> Paul and Barnabas … said, "It was necessary that the Word of God should be spoken to you [the Jews] first; but since you reject it, and judge yourselves as unworthy, … behold, we turn to the Gentiles." —Acts 13:46

Devotional 44
Israel's Wilderness Journey with God (Moses—Out of Anger—Struck the Rock)

Moses and Aaron gathered the assembly together before the rock; and said to them, "Hear now, you rebels! Must we bring water for you out of this rock?" Then Moses lifted his hand and struck the rock twice with his rod. … The LORD spoke, … "Because you did not believe Me, to hallow Me [revere Me as holy/merciful], … you shall not bring this assembly into the land which I have given them." —Numbers 20:10–12

Though God showed His patience and mercy once again, Moses lost his patience with Israel, spoke angrily to them, and struck the rock twice with the rod instead of speaking to it. It was like striking the face of Yahweh (the Rock) all over again. Instead of being the instrument (spokesman) of God to the people, Moses took it upon himself to bring water to them his own way—angrily and without mercy. God wanted to show mercy to His people even though they constantly complained.

The punishment God gave to Moses and Aaron was severe. They too would not enter Canaan but also die in the wilderness even after faithfully leading the people from Egypt to where they were. The Bible does not say that they begged God to take away the punishment, but I am sure they were greatly sorrowful for their sin. Though they did not obey God in this instance, God was merciful, and in time, they entered the eternal land of promise—heaven.

Our Earthly Journey with Jesus (Our Way—Anger—Bad Testimony)

Then Simon Peter, having a sword, drew it and struck the high priest's servant, and cut off his right ear. … So Jesus said to Peter, "Put your sword into the sheath. Shall I not drink the cup which My Father has given Me?"
—John 18:10–11

On the night before Jesus was to be crucified, a mob came with Judas Iscariot to arrest Jesus. Peter became hostile with them and out of impatience and anger set a bad example for Jesus' enemies and disciples. With his sword, he cut off the ear of the high priest's servant. Jesus scolded Peter, telling him that His arrest was part of God's plan. In Luke 22:50–51, we read that Jesus touched the man's ear and healed him. He patiently and lovingly showed the mob and His disciples mercy.

What about You?
Anger means "displeasure, hostility, wrath." Though God is displeased (angry) with your sin, He showed you mercy through Christ. At times, you might become impatient with others and set a bad example of what God is like. This includes how you interact with friends and enemies. Jesus' example is patient mercy. What is your response to others—impatient anger or patient mercy?

Prayer
Father in heaven, forgive our anger, and thank You for Your mercy. Help us interact with our friends, and the not so friendly, with patience and mercy so that our example shows Your holiness, love, mercy, and grace through Christ. In Jesus' name we pray, amen.

Verse of the Week/Day

While we were still sinners, Christ died for us. Much more then, having now been justified by His blood, we shall be saved from [the] wrath [of God] through Him. … We were reconciled to God through the death of His Son, much more, having been reconciled, we shall be saved by His life. —Romans 5:8–10

Devotional 45
Israel's Wilderness Journey with God (Israel Sins—God Sent Biting Serpents)
> The people spoke against God and ... Moses. ... So the LORD sent fiery serpents ... and they bit the people; and many ... died. Therefore the people came to Moses, and said, "We have sinned; ... pray to the LORD that He take away the serpents from us." So Moses prayed for the people. —Numbers 21:5–7

After being in the wilderness for almost forty years, God began leading the Israelites back to Canaan, but they had to go around Edom and Moab to get there, which caused them to become very discouraged. They no longer had the water from the rock; thus, the Israelites grumbled again about that and the manna, which the Bible says they detested. God immediately sent poisonous snakes, and they began suffering the consequences of their sin. The people knew they had done wrong and admitted their sin to Moses before he prayed for their forgiveness. The people were finally taking responsibility for their sin.

Our Earthly Journey with Jesus (We Sin—God Allows the Serpent to Bite)
> [Jesus] began to wash the disciples' feet. ... Peter said to Him, "You shall never wash my feet!" Jesus answered him, "If I do not wash you, you have no part with Me." Simon Peter said to Him, "Lord, not my feet only, but also my hands and my head!" Jesus said to him, "He who is bathed needs only to wash his feet, but is completely clean; and you are clean, but not all of you." —John 13:5–10

Jesus got up to wash the feet of the disciples. When He came to Peter, Peter told Jesus, "You shall never wash my feet." He was too proud to have his feet washed by the humble Master. Pride is evil. Satan—the Serpent, because of pride in his own angelic beauty and his desire to be worshipped in place of God, suffered the consequences of his rebellion and was thrown out of heaven, and has been opposed to God and those *in Christ* ever since.

Judas Iscariot, who was about to betray Jesus, was bitten by Satan and would soon suffer the consequences of his sin. Since Judas was not convicted by Jesus' Words at the supper (Passover) table, God allowed him to succumb to Satan's bite and Judas hung himself. Peter sinned and was also bitten by the Serpent. In contrast, Peter was convicted by Jesus' Words, and suffering the possibility of having no part *in Christ*, instantly admitted his sin. Jesus declared Peter was clean—forgiven.

What about You?
Serpent means "creature opposed to God." One of the hardest things you and I struggle with is repentance—having inward sorrow for sin. But even harder is admitting (confessing) you are a sinner and saying you are sorry you have sinned against God and are in need of His forgiveness. When you sin, God allows the serpents (consequences) of this world to bite, to daily bring you to repentance. Are you convicted by the Holy Spirit? Have you prayed, asking for forgiveness? Confess sin today.

Prayer
Father in heaven, we admit that we have sinned against You and others in so many ways—our thoughts, words, and actions. We ask You to forgive us and keep us from sin. Thank You for convicting us of sin through the Holy Spirit, causing us to repent through the consequences we suffer for sin, and cleansing us through the blood of Christ. In Jesus' name we pray, amen.

Verse of the Week/Day
> The LORD God said to the serpent: ... "I will put enmity [opposition] between you and the woman, between your seed and her Seed; He shall bruise your head, and you shall bruise His heel." —Genesis 3:14–15

Devotional 46
Israel's Wilderness Journey with God (Look at the Snake for Healing—Snakes Not Removed)

> Then the LORD said to Moses, "Make a fiery serpent, and set it on a pole; and it shall be that everyone who is bitten, when he [anyone] looks at it, shall live." So Moses made a bronze serpent, and put it on a pole; … if a serpent had bitten anyone, when he [they] looked at the bronze serpent, he [they] lived. —Numbers 21:8–9

In the last devotional, we learned that the Israelites had repented of their sin against God and that Moses prayed that God would forgive them and take away the snakes. But God did not take away the snakes or their bite. Instead, He told Moses to set up the rod with a snake made of bronze/brass so that the people, after they had been bitten, could look at it and be healed (live). Of course, those who refused to look at it would die. The snakes had been in the wilderness the whole time the Israelites were traveling, but God had kept them at bay. Now they had to live with the consequences of their sin (the snakes and their bite). Thus, the pole with the bronze snake came along with them the rest of the way to Canaan as a reminder that they had to depend on God and obey His Word because all throughout the journey, they had repeatedly complained and come against God and the leadership. When they arrived in Canaan, the Promised Land, the bronze snake was no longer needed. In 2 Kings 18:4, Hezekiah destroyed the bronze snake because it was being worshipped as an idol.

Our Earthly Journey with Jesus (Look at the Cross for Healing—Not Removed from the World)

> [Jesus speaking] "And as Moses lifted up the serpent in the wilderness, even so must the Son of Man be lifted up, that whoever believes in [on (KJV)] Him [Jesus] should not perish but have eternal life." —John 3:14–15

> "I do not pray that You [Father] should take them out of the world, but that You should keep them from the evil one." —John 17:15

Lifting the snake in the wilderness was a picture of Jesus being lifted up on the cross. All who look upon that cross and believe on Jesus will be healed and given eternal life. But that does not mean our problems will be gone in this world. We remain in this sinful environment until we die and suffer the consequences of sin even though we are no longer of the world.

What about You?
Healing means "to restore to full health, forgiveness." God never lets go of you, but sometimes, your relationship with Him is fractured by your disobedience of His will, so God sends reminders of His love for you through discipline. God wants your relationship with Him restored to full health, and tells you to simply look upon the cross of Christ for healing—forgiveness. The cross removed your sin's penalty—eternal death.

Prayer
Father in heaven, daily we break our communion with You by sinning. We know You love us because You send us reminders through discipline. Help us look at the cross of Jesus for healing and forgiveness so that we will be restored to a right relationship with You. We look forward to heaven, communion with You that will never be broken. In Jesus' name we pray, amen.

Verse of the Week/Day

> Bless the LORD, O my soul, and forget not all His benefits: who forgives all your iniquities [sins], who heals all your diseases. —Psalm 103:2–3

Devotional 47
Israel's Wilderness Journey with God (Israel Was Blessed—Could not Be Cursed)
> God said to Balaam, "You shall not go with them; you shall not curse the people, for they are blessed." ... "Behold, I have received a command to bless; He has blessed, I cannot reverse it." —Numbers 22:12–23:20

Balak, the king of Moab, was deeply afraid of the children of Israel because he had heard all the things that the LORD had done to bring them thus far on their journey. So he hired Balaam, a magician, to curse Israel and possibly defeat them through sorcery. But God was watching and intervened in miraculous ways. By an angel and through the speech of Balaam's talking donkey, God told Balaam that he could not curse what the LORD had blessed.

All the Israelites were blessed by God when they went through the baptism in the Red Sea. Though they often sinned, they were still *in Yahweh/Christ*. Look at the biblical account of Adam and Eve. When God made them, He blessed them. When they sinned, He did not curse them. Instead, He cursed the serpent and the ground. Adam and Eve suffered the consequences of their sin with pain and toil but not separation from God. In fact, God came looking for them, sacrificed an animal to clothe them, and covered their sin/nakedness. It does not even say that they repented beforehand. By grace, God kept His promise of blessing! The LORD always keeps His promises!

Our Earthly Journey with Jesus (For Those Who Are Blessed—No Curse)
> He [Jesus] said to Thomas, "Reach your finger here, ... look at My hands; and reach your hand here, ... put it into My side. Do not be unbelieving, but believing. ... Blessed are those who have not seen and yet have believed." —John 20:27–29

Whoever has been given salvation is blessed. In John 13 and 15, Jesus told the disciples they were clean/blessed, except one, Judas Iscariot. Peter had denied Jesus three times, and Thomas doubted Jesus' resurrection and did not believe until he saw Him face to face. Neither he nor Peter were cursed because they were clean/blessed, cleansed by the blood of Christ. Judas Iscariot was not *in Christ* and turned his back on Jesus. Because Judas was not clean/blessed, God allowed Satan to enter him.

What about You?
Blessed means "those receiving God's favor." God cannot go back on His promise that He would be your God and you would be His child—His chosen one—favored by His grace alone. Once you are *in Christ*, you cannot be cursed/rejected. Once you have His grace, you cannot be forsaken. Nothing can separate you from God's love. You are blessed and His forever!

Prayer
Father in heaven, You have shown us Your favor—Your blessing through grace that cleanses us with the blood of Jesus. Thank You that because we are now *in Christ*, nothing can separate us from Your love. We are forever Yours and forever grateful. In Jesus' name we pray, amen.

Verse of the Week/Day
> Who shall bring a charge against God's elect [chosen]? It is God who justifies. Who is he who condemns? ... [Nothing] shall be able to separate us from the love of God which is in Jesus Christ our Lord.
> —Romans 8:33–39

Devotional 48
Israel's Wilderness Journey with God (Two and a Half Tribes Stayed in the Wilderness)
"Let this land be given to your servants as a possession. Do not take us over the Jordan." —Numbers 32:5

They were unfaithful to the God of their fathers, and played the harlot after the gods of the peoples of the land, whom God had destroyed before them. So the God of Israel stirred up the spirit of … [the] king of Assyria. He carried the Reubenites, the Gadites, and the half-tribe of Manasseh into captivity. —1 Chronicles 5:25–26

God had blessed the second generation of Israelites from Egypt through Balaam, but two and a half tribes of Israel did not want to enter Canaan. According to Numbers 32:5, they wanted to stay in the wilderness. Their excuse for staying back was because of the abundance of land for grazing their animals, which they had many of. Through Moses, God allowed them to stay on the east side of the Jordan, but warned them about turning to the idols of the land they wanted to possess. Before the men of war from these two and a half tribes could settle east of the Jordan River, they had to help the rest of Israel conquer Canaan. (Just a note: in devotional 51, all Israel crossed—passed through—the Jordan, except for the wives and children of the two and a half tribes. They had already settled (stayed back) in the land east of the river. This included all those forty years old and younger, who had not been born when the Israelites passed through the baptism of the Red Sea. They were lured by the residents and turned from God, and their children's children were taken into captivity).

Our Earthly Journey with Jesus (Some Want to Stay Back in the World)
He [Jesus] said, … "It is the Spirit who gives life; the flesh profits nothing. The words … I speak … are spirit, and they are life." … Many of His disciples [those taught by Jesus but not *in Christ,* those who were unbelieving] went back and walked with Him no more. —John 6:61–66

Again, many of the people who followed Jesus from place to place were interested only in getting their temporal needs taken care of. They were not interested in the spiritual things Jesus was teaching them. They did not believe Jesus was their Lord and Savior sent from God. Spiritually, they did not pass through from death to life. They were easily lured back to the ways of the world and stopped following Him. Their unbelief cost them and their children the glorious future of eternal life with Jesus.

What about You?
To *stay* means "to hold back." Does unbelief hold you and your children back? Is love for the world—lured by the temporal things it has to offer—going to cause your children to turn from God? Have you obeyed God's covenant and obediently baptized your children by faith and taught them the spiritual things of God? Your obedience/disobedience will impact future generations.

Prayer
Father, we know that our obedience/disobedience to Your Word will impact our children, grandchildren, and beyond. Help us not be lured by the temporal things this world has to offer, but trust You alone, for our children's sake. In Jesus' name, amen.

Verse of the Week/Day
For I do not want you to be ignorant ⋅ … brothers and sisters, that our ancestors were *all* under the cloud, and that they *all* passed through the sea. They were *all* baptized into [unto (NKJV)] Moses in the cloud [Holy Spirit] and in the sea [water]. They *all* … drank the same spiritual drink; for they drank from the spiritual Rock that accompanied them, and that Rock was Christ. —1 Corinthians 10:1–4 (NIV); emphasis added

Devotional 49
Israel's Wilderness Journey with God (God's Promises on Israel's Journey)

> The LORD spoke to Joshua, … saying: … "Arise, go over this Jordan, you and all this people, to the land which I am giving … the children of Israel. … I will be with you. I will not leave you nor forsake you. Be strong and of good courage, for to this people you shall divide as an inheritance the land which I swore to their fathers to give them." —Joshua 1:1–6

Through Moses, God had led the children of Israel from Egypt to the border of Canaan and promised to never leave or forsake them. That promise He had kept even though the Israelites had tested and sinned against Him repeatedly. God was giving the new leader, Joshua, and the next generation of Israelites, the long-awaited Promised Land—Canaan, the land from Egypt to Assyria, the Jordan River to the Mediterranean Sea. God promised to conquer the land through Joshua (another name for Jesus). No one would stand in their way because He had already defeated their enemies. Though the people would be spread out over all the land of Canaan, each with a piece of land that had been prepared for them to be their inheritance, they were not to be afraid because His presence would always be with them. God's presence was going to be shown through Joshua's leadership, the seventy judges, and the ark of the covenant at the tabernacle, which the people visited once a year on the Day of Atonement, when the high priest came into the presence of God, in the holy of holies, to offer the sacrifice for the atonement of all their sins.

Our Earthly Journey with Jesus (God's Promises on Our Journey)

> "I [Jesus] go to prepare a place for you. And if I go and prepare a place for you, I will come again and receive you to Myself; that where I am, there you may be also. … The Helper, the Holy Spirit, whom the Father will send in My name, He will teach you all things, and bring to your remembrance all things that I said to you."
> —John 14:2–3 & 26

God promised us that He has already prepared a place for us and has defeated Satan, this world, and our sinful nature. He has given us peace with Himself through Jesus, our Lord and Savior. As long as we are in this world, we do not need to be afraid because we always have the Holy Spirit in us, helping us to remember everything God's Word teaches us. Through His power, the Holy Spirit continually works to sanctify us and help us to respond with obedience to the Word of God—Jesus.

What about You?
Promise means "to assure/guarantee." The promised Holy Spirit is God's guaranteed presence. With the Holy Spirit, you are assured that God's promise of preparing a place in eternity with Jesus is already a reality.

Prayer
Father in heaven, thank You for the promise of heaven You give us as Your children, Your chosen ones, through the Holy Spirit, and for the assurance that Your constant presence is with us now on earth and for all eternity. In Jesus' name, amen.

Verse of the Week/Day

> We, according to His promise, look for new heavens and a new earth in which righteousness dwells.
> —2 Peter 3:13

> God … has … given us the Spirit in our hearts as a guarantee. —2 Corinthians 1:21–22

Devotional 50
Israel's Wilderness Journey with God (Obedience—Response to God's Promises)

> [God speaking] "Be strong and very courageous. Be careful to obey all the law my servant Moses gave you; do not turn from it to the right or to the left, … meditate on it day and night." —Joshua 1:7–8 (NIV)

> … The people said to Joshua, "The LORD our God we will serve, and His voice we will obey!" —Joshua 24:24

God was speaking and working through Joshua, the Israelites' new leader. When Joshua brought the Word of God to the Israelites, they promised obedience in response. God had given the Israelites through Moses the moral law (the Ten Commandments), the social laws (Leviticus), and many other ordinances to live His way in obedience. The people were going to be spread out all over the land of Canaan. That meant they would not always be in the presence of Joshua or the ark in the tabernacle, but since they settled in Canaan as family units, each unit had a leader or judge filled with the Holy Spirit. God's Word was now written down so that it could be read. (It is possible that there was more than one copy of God's Word, but the Bible does not give that detail.) The LORD wanted them to meditate on His Word day and night to keep them from forgetting and falling away from the love He had for them. He promised He would be with them wherever they went.

Our Earthly Journey with Jesus (Obedience—Response to God's Promises)

> Jesus replied, "Anyone who loves me will obey my teaching. My Father will love them, and we will come to them and make our home with them." —John 14:23 (NIV)

God is Love and commands obedience. Obedience shows love for God. Love and obedience are the most important responses to God's commands. In Mark 12:30–31, Jesus told His disciples to love God with all their heart, soul, mind, and strength, and to love their neighbors as themselves—as He had loved them. Jesus promised to make His home in us, His disciples, and make us one *in Him*. Only through the love and obedience of Christ in our lives, can we respond with love and obedience toward God and others.

What about You?
Respond means "to answer, reply." When God's Word comes to you, a response of obedience and thanksgiving is needed. You are to answer/reply by offering yourself to Him obediently, walking by the faith and obedience of Christ, and offer yourself thankfully; loving, praising, and serving Him. Obedience is always submission to someone else's will. For us, it is God's Will. We are His instruments for His use.

Prayer
Father in heaven, sometimes, we do not respond with love for You or our neighbors. Help us to respond with love and obedience; submitting to Your will, walking by the faith of Christ and His obedience, and offering ourselves by thankfully loving, praising, and serving You all our life. Thank You for establishing Your home in us and making us one *in You*. In Jesus' name we pray, amen.

Verse of the Week/Day

> The fruit of the Spirit is love, joy, peace, longsuffering [patience], kindness, goodness, faithfulness, gentleness, self-control [temperance (KJV)]. Against such there is no law. Those who are Christ's have crucified the flesh with its passions and desires. If we live in the Spirit, let us also walk in the Spirit. —Galatians 5:22–25

Devotional 51
Israel's Wilderness Journey with God (New Generation Blessed with Canaan)
> The waters … were cut off; and the people crossed over opposite Jericho. … The priests who bore the ark of the covenant of the LORD stood firm on dry ground in the midst of the Jordan; and all Israel [except those who settled east of the Jordan] crossed over on dry ground, until all the people had crossed completely over the Jordan. —Joshua 3:16–17

God blessed the second generation, those forty years old and younger, with baptism, thus fulfilling His promise to the next generation. God miraculously stopped the flooded Jordan River as they, along with their parents (who were forty to sixty years old), passed through the Jordan into the Promised Land. Joshua—meaning Yahweh/Jesus Is Salvation—led them. They were protected by the ark of the covenant (God's Word/Law), which the priests held in the midst of the river until all were in Canaan.

Our Earthly Journey with Jesus (Future Generations Blessed with Abundant Life)
> "I do not pray for these alone, but also for those who will believe in [on (KJV)] Me through their word; that they all may be one, as You, Father, are in Me, and I in You; that they also may be one in Us, that the world may believe that You sent Me." —John 17:20–21

Jesus was praying for those who believed as well as those He would call in due time including those not yet born. The purpose for His prayer was to make all who believed one *in Him*. He is also praying for your/His children (Ezekiel 16:20–22) and promising abundant life to future generations of those who are already *in Him*.

What about You?
Life means "living abundantly/eternally." There is only one way to have abundant/eternal life, and that is to have Christ in you. If you are *in Christ*, so are your/His children (see Ezekiel above). They have already been baptized spiritually by the Holy Spirit and are *in Christ* and part of the covenant promise, but have your/His children passed through the water (been baptized physically) as were the Israelites who crossed the Jordan? Is God still waiting for you to trust and obey Him completely and publicly? The Bible says that because you are *in Christ*, your children are already holy/sanctified (See 1 Corinthians 7:14). God promises to bless your children and your children's children for generations to come if you abide *in Christ*. Will you baptize your children, not for their salvation (because they are already *in Christ*) but by faith, believing they are already in the covenant?

Prayer
Father, Your promise is for us and our children. Help us to obey so that our children may be blessed. In Jesus' name, amen.

Verse of the Week/Day
> They shall be My people, and I will be their God; then I will give them one heart and one way, that they may fear Me forever, for the good of them and their children after them. And I will make an everlasting covenant with them, that I will not turn away from doing them good; but I will put My fear in their hearts so that they will not depart from Me. —Jeremiah 32:38–40

> Peter said to them, "Repent, and let every one of you be baptized in the name of Jesus Christ for the remission of sins; and you shall receive the gift of the Holy Spirit. For the promise is to you and to your children, and to all who are afar off, as many as the Lord our God will call." —Acts 2:38–39

Devotional 52
Israel's Wilderness Journey with God (God Carried Israel to the End)

> I will mention … the great goodness toward the house of Israel, which He has bestowed on them according to His mercies. … He [the LORD] became their Savior. In all their affliction He was afflicted, and the Angel of His Presence saved them; in His love and in His pity He redeemed them; and He bore them and carried them all the days of old. —Isaiah 63:7–9

All through Israel's wilderness journey from Egypt to Canaan, God carried them. It was God who lifted them up when they were bowed down because of their slavery in Egypt. It was God who delivered them from their bondage through supernatural plagues. It was God who redeemed them when they went through the Red Sea on dry ground. It was God who mercifully loved them and showed patience when they complained. Finally, it was God who gave rest to all—from the youngest to the oldest—in the Promised Land, Canaan. The LORD bore their afflictions, sickness, suffering, trouble, and pain as if they were His own.

Our Earthly Journey with Jesus (Jesus Carries Us to the End)

> And He [Jesus], bearing [carrying] His cross, went out to a place called the Place of a Skull, which is called in Hebrew, Golgotha, where they crucified Him. —John 19:17–18

The phrase *carrying His own cross* refers to "For He [God] made Him [Jesus], who knew no sin, to be sin for us, that we might become the righteousness of God *in Him*" (2 Corinthians 5:21; emphasis added). He took our place and carried our guilt of sin in His body upon the cross. We are eternally healed, and our sin is completely erased. Hallelujah! What an awesome Savior!

What about You?
To *carry* means "to take upon one's self someone else's burdens." All through your journey from conception/regeneration (the indwelling of the Holy Spirit) to your physical death, Jesus has and will carry you to the end. He has shown you His faithfulness by keeping His promises/covenant and caused you to trust Him to carry you through your baptism (new birth) by true faith. Jesus took on Himself your infirmities and sorrows by bearing on the cross the punishment of your sin that you deserved, and granted you repentance and forgiveness that saved you from being eternally separated from God.

Through Jesus' suffering, God declared you spiritually justified and right with Him. He reconciled you by restoring your relationship with Him and adopted you as His child, making you an heir of heaven. He works every day to sanctify you by the Holy Spirit to make your mortal body more and more holy. He will never leave you or forsake you during this journey on earth. Then at the end of time, you will finally be glorified, completely molded into the image of Christ, perfect *in Him* for all eternity.

Prayer
Father in heaven, through the Holy Spirit, You have faithfully kept Your promise and have carried us all the way through our journey of life with You. We owe all our life, love, obedience, and thanksgiving to You. In the glorious name of our Lord and Savior, Jesus Christ, we pray, amen.

Verse of the Week/Day

> Listen to Me, O house of Jacob, and all the remnant of the house of Israel [all those *in Christ*], who have been upheld by Me from birth, who have been carried from the womb: even to your old age, I am He, and even to gray hairs I will carry you! I have made, and I will bear; even I will carry, and will deliver you. —Isaiah 46:3–4

Jacob's Family in Egypt (Seventy Persons) and in the Exodus (Seventy Family Units Leaving Egypt)

1. Columns 1 and 3 (names in black on the following page) are the offspring of Jacob that went to Egypt from Canaan. There are sixty-nine offspring plus Jacob; a total of seventy persons. All are males except a daughter (Dinah) and a granddaughter (Serah). The twelve sons of Jacob are in bold (twelve tribes).

2. The spouses are not counted, only the offspring (bloodline of Jacob) are counted.

3. Dinah was not a tribe, and Serah was not a family unit. They either married into another family or remained single.

4. All came from Canaan except Joseph and his two sons, Ephraim and Manasseh (who were already in Egypt).

5. Columns 2 and 4 (names in red) are the seventy family units that left Egypt to go back to Canaan. This is where the seventy elders came from, one representative from each family unit.

6. The numbers twelve and seventy were complete numbers in the Bible, thus the twelve tribes and seventy family units/elders.

7. In the Old Testament, the seventy elders were judges under the leadership of Moses and Aaron, the high priest. In the New Testament, the Sanhedrin (or council) was made up of seventy elders with the high priest presiding.

8. Reuben was the oldest of Jacob's sons but did not get the birthright because he sinned against Jacob.

9. Instead, Jacob gave the birthright to Joseph, the oldest son of Rachel. (Birthright means "a double inheritance.") Thus, the tribe of Joseph (names in green) became two tribes—the tribe of Ephraim and the tribe of Mannaseh.

10. Zelopnehad (son of Hepher), who was from the tribe of Mannaseh, had no sons. His five daughters asked Moses for an inheritance to carry on the family name. They were granted their request if they married within the tribe.

11. The tribe of Levi (names in blue) discontinued being called a tribe (they had no inheritance in the land of Canaan). Instead, they were set aside by God through Moses to serve in the tabernacle and bring the Word of God to Israel. The sons of Amram became the priests, and the rest of the family of Levi became the Levites. (They lived in towns and cities.)

12. Because the tribe of Levi had no inheritance (land to grow crops and raise livestock), the tithes and offerings of grain and animals from the other tribes supported the priests and Levites and their families.

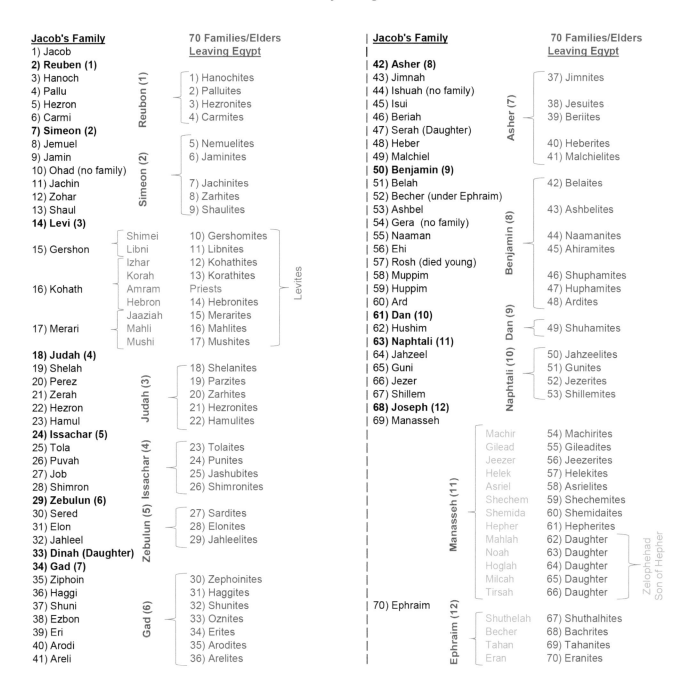

Jacob's Family
1) Jacob
2) Reuben (1)
3) Hanoch
4) Pallu
5) Hezron
6) Carmi
7) Simeon (2)
8) Jemuel
9) Jamin
10) Ohad (no family)
11) Jachin
12) Zohar
13) Shaul
14) Levi (3)
15) Gershon
16) Kohath
17) Merari
18) Judah (4)
19) Shelah
20) Perez
21) Zerah
22) Hezron
23) Hamul
24) Issachar (5)
25) Tola
26) Puvah
27) Job
28) Shimron
29) Zebulun (6)
30) Sered
31) Elon
32) Jahleel
33) Dinah (Daughter)
34) Gad (7)
35) Ziphoin
36) Haggi
37) Shuni
38) Ezbon
39) Eri
40) Arodi
41) Areli

70 Families/Elders Leaving Egypt

Reubon (1)
1) Hanochites
2) Palluites
3) Hezronites
4) Carmites

Simeon (2)
5) Nemuelites
6) Jaminites
7) Jachinites
8) Zarhites
9) Shaulites

Levites
Shimei — 10) Gershomites
Libni — 11) Libnites
Izhar — 12) Kohathites
Korah — 13) Korathites
Amram — Priests
Hebron — 14) Hebronites
Jaaziah — 15) Merarites
Mahli — 16) Mahlites
Mushi — 17) Mushites

Judah (3)
18) Shelanites
19) Parzites
20) Zarhites
21) Hezronites
22) Hamulites

Issachar (4)
23) Tolaites
24) Punites
25) Jashubites
26) Shimronites

Zebulun (5)
27) Sardites
28) Elonites
29) Jahleelites

Gad (6)
30) Zephoinites
31) Haggites
32) Shunites
33) Oznites
34) Erites
35) Arodites
36) Arelites

Jacob's Family
42) Asher (8)
43) Jimnah
44) Ishuah (no family)
45) Isui
46) Beriah
47) Serah (Daughter)
48) Heber
49) Malchiel
50) Benjamin (9)
51) Belah
52) Becher (under Ephraim)
53) Ashbel
54) Gera (no family)
55) Naaman
56) Ehi
57) Rosh (died young)
58) Muppim
59) Huppim
60) Ard
61) Dan (10)
62) Hushim
63) Naphtali (11)
64) Jahzeel
65) Guni
66) Jezer
67) Shillem
68) Joseph (12)
69) Manasseh

70) Ephraim

70 Families/Elders Leaving Egypt

Asher (7)
37) Jimnites
38) Jesuites
39) Beriites
40) Heberites
41) Malchielites

Benjamin (8)
42) Belaites
43) Ashbelites
44) Naamanites
45) Ahiramites
46) Shuphamites
47) Huphamites
48) Ardites

Dan (9)
49) Shuhamites

Naphtali (10)
50) Jahzeelites
51) Gunites
52) Jezerites
53) Shillemites

Manasseh (11)
Machir — 54) Machirites
Gilead — 55) Gileadites
Jeezer — 56) Jeezerites
Helek — 57) Helekites
Asriel — 58) Asrielites
Shechem — 59) Shechemites
Shemida — 60) Shemidaites
Hepher — 61) Hepherites
Mahlah — 62) Daughter
Noah — 63) Daughter
Hoglah — 64) Daughter
Milcah — 65) Daughter
Tirsah — 66) Daughter
Zelophehad Son of Hepher

Ephraim (12)
Shuthelah — 67) Shuthalhites
Becher — 68) Bachrites
Tahan — 69) Tahanites
Eran — 70) Eranites

Exodus (Forty Camps): A Biblical Complete Number

-Moses had the encounter with the burning bush at Mount Sinai. Here is a summary of the biblical story of the Exodus.
-At the beginning of the story of the Exodus from Egypt, God sent Aaron to meet Moses at Mount Sinai in Midian (Arabia).

Leaving Egypt
    Egypt: Leviticus 23:5. First month (Abib [March–April]), fourteenth day of the month. At twilight, the Israelites celebrated the first Passover (Saturday).

                Exodus 12:37–13:7. Left Rameses on the fifteenth day of the month and ate unleavened bread for the next seven days (Sunday-Saturday) (seven days' journey).

In the Desert
1) Succoth: Exodus 13:17-18. Arrived on the twenty-second day of the month. They went by way of the sea.
2) Etham: Exodus 13:20. Went along the Red Sea and arrived in Etham, the end of the desert.
3) Pi Hahiroth: Exodus 14:1-2. Between Migdol and Etham, opposite from Baal Zephon.
   • Exodus 14:3ff. This is where Israel crossed the Red Sea after three weeks of traveling.
   • It took all night to cross on the ten-mile path through the sea (Straits of Tiran?).
   • They entered the wilderness of Shur in Arabia (Midian) (Galatians 4:25).

In the Wilderness
4) Marah: Exodus 15:22-25. Traveled three days to Marah with no water. The water was bitter (Israel was tested).
5) Elim: Exodus 15:27. Twelve fountains of water, seventy palm trees (twelve tribes and seventy family units).
6) Wilderness of Sin: Exodus 16A. Next to the Red Sea, south of Mount Sinai in Arabia.
7) Dophkah: Exodus 16:1Bff. (Fifteenth day of the second month) Quail and manna (first Sabbath observed).
8) Alush: Exodus 17:1. Moses spent a week teaching Israel to obey and depend on God (Numbers 33:13).
9) Rephidim: Exodus 17:6-7. By Horeb (no water), they struck the rock and received water continuously for a year.
   • Exodus 17:8-16. Amalekites (descendants of Esau/Edom) fought against Israel (rested one month).
   • Exodus 18:1ff. Jethro (Moses' father-in-law) and family reunited with Moses.

At Mount Sinai
10) Mount Sinai: Exodus 19:1. (Third month, fourteenth day) stayed there eleven months.
   • Exodus 20:1ff. Ten Commandments/worshipping the gold calf.
   • Leviticus 1:1ff. All the laws, tabernacle, and priesthood established.
   • Numbers 9:1-5. Celebrated Passover after tabernacle completed (year two, first month, fourteenth day).

Leaving Mount Sinai
11) Kibroth Hattaavah: Numbers 11:31-3. Left Sinai (second year, second month, twentieth day). Quail sent.
12) Hazeroth: Numbers 12:9-10. Moses' leadership was attacked. Miriam punished with leprosy (stayed a week).

Wilderness of Paran
13) Rithmah
14) Rimmon Perez
15) Libnah
16) Rissah
17) Kehelathah
18) Mount Shepher
19) Haradah
20) Makheloth

Activities around Mount Sinai	-Leviticus, Numbers (Laws taught and obeyed)
	-Numbers 1 (Perhaps two million people counted)
	-Numbers 2 (Israel camped around the tabernacle by tribe)
	-Numbers 3 & 4 (Levites work established)
	-Numbers 5, 6, 7, 8 (Social regulations)
	-Numbers 11:16 (Seventy elders/judges chosen)
	-Numbers 18:1ff (Tithes & offerings from increase)

Exodus (Forty Camps): A Biblical Complete Number

21) Tahath	Wilderness	-Deut. 1:33 (God's presence/cloud by day/fire by night)
22) Terah	Wanderings	-Deut. 2:7 (Israel lacked nothing for forty years in the wilderness)
23) Mithkah		-Deut. 6:1-15 (Instructions to teach next generation)
24) Hashmonah		-Deut. 7:16-24 (God promises to protect Israel from enemies)
25) Maseroth		-Deut. 8:2 (God humbled and tested them)
26) Bene Jaakah		-Deut. 8:3 (Manna/water for forty years)
27) Hor Hagidgad		-Deut. 8:4 (Garments did not wear out; feet did not swell up)
28) Jotbathah		-Deut. 28:1ff (Blessing for obedience/curses for disobedience)
29) Abronah		-Deut. 29:5 (Shoes did not wear out)
30) Ezion Geber		-Deut. 32 and 33 (Moses' song and final blessing)

Wilderness of Zin

31) Kadesh: Sent out spies (second year, third month, first day). (Numbers 13:1-2).
- Numbers 14:1ff. People disobeyed, and Amalekites and Canaanites defeated rebel Israelites.
    - The Israelites did not put their trust in God, so they had to stay in the wilderness forty years.
    - All those who were twenty years old and older died (with two exceptions: Joshua and Caleb).
- Numbers 16. Korah, Dathan, and Abiram rebelled against Moses and Aaron.
- Numbers 20:1. Miriam died at Kadesh.
- Numbers 20:1-11. Moses disobeyed and struck the rock instead of speaking to it at Kadesh.
- Numbers 20:12. Because of their disobedience, Moses and Aaron could not go into Canaan.
- Numbers 20:14ff. In the fortieth year, God began to lead the people back to the Promised Land starting from the wilderness of Zin (Kadesh).

Leaving Kadesh for Canaan

32) Mount Hor: Aaron died and was buried on Mount Hor (Numbers 20:22-28).
33) Zalmonah: Moses did not go through Edom; instead, he went around Edom (Numbers 20:14-21).
34) Punon: Venomous snakes; needed to look at brass snake for healing, believing (Numbers 21:4-9).
35) Oboth: On the southeast side of Edom (Children of Esau) (Numbers 21:10).
36) Ije Abarim: On the eastern border of Moab (Children of Lot) (Numbers 21:11).
37) Diban Gad: Located in the Zered Valley (Numbers 21:12).
38) Almon Diblotham: Went west to Canaan along the Arnon River (Numbers 21:13).
39) Abirim/Nebo: Israel defeated Sihon and Og (Numbers 21:21-35). (Numbers 22-24)
40) Jordan River: Balak of Moab wanted Balaam to Curse Israel. God intervened and Balaam blessed Israel.

Entering Canaan
- Numbers 27:12-23. Joshua was chosen to lead Israel into the Promised Land.
- Deuteronomy 1-33. Moses' instructions to the second generation of Israel from Egypt.
- Deuteronomy 34:1-7. Moses died on Mount Nebo after seeing Canaan from mountaintop.
- Joshua 3:14-17. Israel crossed the Jordan miraculously.
- Joshua 5:2-9. Males circumcised according to the command the Lord gave Abraham.
- Joshua 5:10. In year 41 (first month, fourteenth day) the Israelites celebrated the Passover.
- Joshua 5:12. Manna stopped because Israel started eating the produce of Canaan.

Afterwords

It is not our striving but God who draws us to Himself. We simply respond with obedience, and through faith, we trust in God's ability to fulfill all His promises; to keep us close; to nurture, comfort, and strengthen us; and to carry us to the end.

Whatever good comes from us, we must realize that it does not originate in us but is the work of the Holy Spirit alone, who purifies us, makes us holy, and performs God's goodness in and through us to bring glory to the Father.

Prayer
Father in heaven, You alone are our God, and we are Your servants. Use us, we pray, as instruments of Your love to glorify Yourself in and through us as we live one day at a time on life's journey with Jesus in this sinful world. Thank You for your goodness to us and for carrying us all the way from the beginning of our lives to the end, here on earth. We are forever grateful. In Jesus' name we pray, amen.

Printed in the United States
By Bookmasters